ARTIFACTS

ARCHAEOLOGIST'S TOOLKIT

SERIES EDITORS: LARRY J. ZIMMERMAN AND WILLIAM GREEN

The Archaeologist's Toolkit is an integrated set of seven volumes designed to teach novice archaeologists and students the basics of doing archaeological fieldwork, analysis, and presentation. Students are led through the process of designing a study, doing survey work, excavating, properly working with artifacts and biological remains, curating their materials, and presenting findings to various audiences. The volumes—written by experienced field archaeologists—are full of practical advice, tips, case studies, and illustrations to help the reader. All of this is done with careful attention to promoting a conservation ethic and an understanding of the legal and practical environment of contemporary American cultural resource laws and regulations. The Toolkit is an essential resource for anyone working in the field and ideal for training archaeology students in classrooms and field schools.

Volume 1: *Archaeology by Design*
By Stephen L. Black and Kevin Jolly

Volume 2: *Archaeological Survey*
By James M. Collins and Brian Leigh Molyneaux

Volume 3: *Excavation*
By David L. Carmichael and Robert Lafferty

Volume 4: *Artifacts*
By Charles R. Ewen

Volume 5: *Archaeobiology*
By Kristin D. Sobolik

**Volume 6: *Curating Archaeological Collections:
From the Field to the Repository***
By Lynne P. Sullivan and S. Terry Childs

Volume 7: *Presenting the Past*
By Larry J. Zimmerman

ARTIFACTS

CHARLES R. EWEN

ARCHAEOLOGIST'S TOOLKIT
VOLUME 4

ALTAMIRA
PRESS

A Division of Rowman & Littlefield Publishers, Inc.
Walnut Creek • Lanham • New York • Oxford

ALTAMIRA PRESS
A Division of Rowman & Littlefield Publishers, Inc.
1630 North Main Street, #367
Walnut Creek, CA 94596
www.altamirapress.com

Rowman & Littlefield Publishers, Inc.
A Member of the Rowman & Littlefield Publishing Group
4501 Forbes Boulevard, Suite 200
Lanham, MD 20706

PO Box 317
Oxford
OX2 9RU, UK

British Library Cataloguing in Publication Information Available

Library of Congress Cataloging-in-Publication Data
Ewen, Charles Robin.
   Artifacts / Charles R. Ewen.
      p. cm. — (Archaeologist's toolkit ; v. 4)
   Includes bibliographical references (p.) and index.
   ISBN 978-0-7591-0022-0
      1. Archaeology—Methodology. 2. Excavations (Archaeology) 3.
   Antiquities—Collection and preservation. 4. Antiquities—Analysis. I. Title.
   II. Series.

   CC75.7 .E97 2003
   930.1'028—dc21

                                                                2002152408
Printed in the United States of America

∞™ The paper used in this publication meets the minimum requirements of
American National Standard for Information Sciences—Permanence of Paper
for Printed Library Materials, ANSI/NISO Z39.48-1992.

CONTENTS

SERIES EDITORS' FOREWORD

The Archaeologist's Toolkit is a series of books on how to plan, design, carry out, and use the results of archaeological research. The series contains seven books written by acknowledged experts in their fields. Each book is a self-contained treatment of an important element of modern archaeology. Therefore, each book can stand alone as a reference work for archaeologists in public agencies, private firms, and museums, as well as a textbook and guidebook for classrooms and field settings. The books function even better as a set, because they are integrated through cross-references and complementary subject matter.

Archaeology is a rapidly growing field, one that is no longer the exclusive province of academia. Today, archaeology is a part of daily life in both the public and private sectors. Thousands of archaeologists apply their knowledge and skills every day to understand the human past. Recent explosive growth in archaeology has heightened the need for clear and succinct guidance on professional practice. Therefore, this series supplies ready reference to the latest information on methods and techniques—the tools of the trade that serve as handy guides for longtime practitioners and essential resources for archaeologists in training.

Archaeologists help solve modern problems: They find, assess, recover, preserve, and interpret the evidence of the human past in light of public interest and in the face of multiple land use and development interests. Most of North American archaeology is devoted to cultural resource management (CRM), so the Archaeologist's Toolkit focuses on practical approaches to solving real problems in CRM and public archaeology. The books contain numerous case studies from all parts of the continent, illustrating the range and diversity of applications. The series emphasizes the importance of such realistic considerations as budgeting, scheduling, and team coordination. In addition, accountability to the public as well as to the profession is a common theme throughout the series.

Volume 1, *Archaeology by Design*, stresses the importance of research design in all phases and at all scales of archaeology. It shows how and why you should develop, apply, and refine research designs. Whether you are surveying quarter-acre cell tower sites or excavating stratified villages with millions of artifacts, your work will be more productive, efficient, and useful if you pay close and continuous attention to your research design.

Volume 2, *Archaeological Survey*, recognizes that most fieldwork in North America is devoted to survey: finding and evaluating archaeological resources. It covers prefield and field strategies to help you maximize the effectiveness and efficiency of archaeological survey. It shows how to choose appropriate strategies and methods ranging from landowner negotiations, surface reconnaissance, and shovel testing to geophysical survey, aerial photography, and report writing.

Volume 3, *Excavation*, covers the fundamentals of dirt archaeology in diverse settings, while emphasizing the importance of ethics during the controlled recovery—and destruction—of the archaeological record. This book shows how to select and apply excavation methods appropriate to specific needs and circumstances and how to maximize useful results while minimizing loss of data.

Volume 4, *Artifacts*, provides students as well as experienced archaeologists with useful guidance on preparing and analyzing artifacts. Both prehistoric- and historic-era artifacts are covered in detail. The discussion and case studies range from processing and cataloging through classification, data manipulation, and specialized analyses of a wide range of artifact forms.

Volume 5, *Archaeobiology*, covers the analysis and interpretation of biological remains from archaeological sites. The book shows how to recover, sample, analyze, and interpret the plant and animal remains most frequently excavated from archaeological sites in North America. Case studies from CRM and other archaeological research illustrate strategies for effective and meaningful use of biological data.

Volume 6, *Curating Archaeological Collections*, addresses a crucial but often ignored aspect of archaeology: proper care of the specimens and records generated in the field and the lab. This book covers strategies for effective short- and long-term collections management. Case studies illustrate the do's and don'ts that you need to know to make the best use of existing collections and to make your own work useful for others.

Volume 7, *Presenting the Past*, covers another area that has not received sufficient attention: communication of archaeology to a variety of audiences. Different tools are needed to present archaeology to other archaeologists, to sponsoring agencies, and to the interested public. This book shows how to choose the approaches and methods to take when presenting technical and nontechnical information through various means to various audiences.

Each of these books and the series as a whole are designed to be equally useful to practicing archaeologists and to archaeology students. Practicing archaeologists in CRM firms, agencies, academia, and museums will find the books useful as reference tools and as brush-up guides on current concerns and approaches. Instructors and students in field schools, lab classes, and short courses of various types will find the series valuable because of each book's practical orientation to problem solving.

As the series editors, we have enjoyed bringing these books together and working with the authors. We thank all of the authors— Steve Black, Dave Carmichael, Terry Childs, Jim Collins, Charlie Ewen, Kevin Jolly, Robert Lafferty, Brian Molyneaux, Kris Sobolik, and Lynne Sullivan—for their hard work and patience. We also offer sincere thanks to Mitch Allen of AltaMira Press and a special acknowledgment to Brian Fagan.

LARRY J. ZIMMERMAN
WILLIAM GREEN

ACKNOWLEDGMENTS

When I was approached a couple of years ago and asked to produce a brief volume on artifact analysis, I was at first startled, then flattered, then dismayed. Dismayed because the series editors wanted a manuscript in nine months! "Take a sabbatical," they told me, as if this were a real option. Nevertheless, I was able to produce a rough draft, close to the deadline. Over the next couple of years, that manuscript bounced around the offices of Altamira Press until it emerged in its present form.

This book represents more of a personal philosophy toward artifact analysis than a "how-to" guide. It has been thirty years in the making, and everyone I have ever worked with or whose work I have read in the field of archaeology has had a hand in shaping it. My gratitude to so many who have helped me to a satisfying career in archaeology is far too long to list individually. However, there are several folk who deserve special mention for their particular help on this volume.

First, the students of my archaeological methods courses over the years are to be commended for providing me with insight into the teaching of artifact analysis. Many helpful comments came out of those classes. I am also indebted to my fellow ECU faculty members Randy Daniel and Jane Eastman (now at Western Carolina University) for looking over the lithic and ceramic analysis sections, respectively. Their comments helped me to better understand the finer points of these analyses. Tricia Samford and Linda Carnes-McNaughton helped to gather important references in North Carolina, and Lela Donat was helpful in obtaining information from the Arkansas Archeological Survey.

The folks at Altamira Press have also been very patient and helpful, even when I was not. Mitch Allen had the most helpful edits of the manuscript, and Grace Ebron and Lynn Weber were terrific during the production phase. I wear their Altamira Press shirt proudly.

Finally, my family (Gretchen, Kate, and Madeline) deserve mention, since several family outings had to be postponed while I worked this text. As I said, many people had a hand in producing this volume, but its shortcomings are solely my responsibility.

PART I

INTRODUCTION

This section provides the rationale for artifact analysis by defining the subject matter (the types of artifacts to be analyzed) and discussing the different perspectives concerning the interpretation of archaeological remains. We begin by defining what an artifact is and what it is not, thus setting the parameters for the remainder of this book. The importance of the concept of context, which provides meaning for the recovered artifacts, cannot be overstressed in the analysis of artifacts. The scope of the artifact assemblage is addressed, and the distinction between prehistoric and historic sites and the different approaches applied to each is noted. The significant role of archaeological theory on artifact analysis is examined, where we specifically note that it appears that the kinds of analyses performed are more a function of the questions being asked, rather than of the various technologies available. Finally, the requirements of legally mandated archaeology (cultural resource management, or CRM) and the implications for artifact analysis are discussed.

1

INTRODUCTION

Indiana Jones, in *Raiders of the Lost Ark*, makes the practice of archaeology seem relatively simple, albeit somewhat dangerous. One merely finds an old artifact or map that leads you to an amazing site, which you pillage at will. Only Nazis and fools spend long hours digging dry holes or carefully recording their finds. (Ironically, I point out in my classes that it was the Nazis who were doing the real archaeology and did the background work that allowed Jones to find the ark!) As long as the artifacts end up in a museum, it doesn't matter how you recovered them or how you arrived at your interpretations. Fortunately, most people can separate fact from fiction, although when I ask students in my introductory "Archaeology around the World" classes to name a famous archaeologist, Indiana Jones is always among the top five.

Fieldwork has always been what defines archaeology in the popular imagination. When the general public thinks about archaeology, they picture weather-beaten individuals laboring with shovels and picks in exotic locales. Even the more enlightened layperson focuses on the field aspects of archaeology. To most people, archaeologists are either working on a dig or writing a book about their exciting finds. The part between the exciting discoveries and the published report receives little, if any, attention.

The profession of archaeology is not immune to such stereotyping. If you ask most archaeologists why they got into the field, the most common answer is *not* "I enjoy endless hours of size-sorting lithic debitage." Go to the bar at any archaeological conference, and you'll likely hear anecdotes pertaining to fieldwork, not artifact analysis.

Yet, it is the analysis of what we find in the field that permits us to do our job: interpreting the past. It is the second most important thing that separates the archaeologist from the pothunter.

Curiously, relatively few books focus strictly on the analysis of the many types of artifacts recovered from archaeological sites. How can this be if this aspect of archaeology is so important? Probably, as I discovered during the preparation of this volume, because the scope of the undertaking is so daunting. There are myriad types of artifacts that archaeologists recover from excavations and countless ways of looking at them. Each question asked of the artifact may require a different analytical method to obtain the desired answer.

Answers obtained by differing methods may differ, but all may be equally valid depending on how they are used. For example, historic ceramics may be dated by applying Stanley South's mean ceramic date formula to raw sherd counts of stylistic types. By a different method of quantification and classification (i.e., calculating minimum vessel counts and a more generic typology), it is possible to approximate the status of the past owner of the same ceramic assemblage using George Miller's CC Index. Both of these methods will be discussed more fully later in this volume.

To "write the book" on artifact analysis demands that the author either be incredibly naive or possess excessive hubris. I have been accused of both. However, this book is not intended to provide the reader with a step-by-step guide to archaeological analysis or the nuts and bolts of the many arcane methods by which artifacts can be examined. Rather, it is meant to provoke the reader into thinking about the complexities of the general task of artifact analysis before embarking on that next endeavor and to provide an overview of some of the more commonly used analytical procedures and some additional source material for more detailed analyses.

2

THE MATERIAL ASSEMBLAGE

Archaeologists, like many scholars, have a bad habit of using the same term in different ways. This is especially true of archaeologists that have been educated at different institutions embracing different paradigms or working for various agencies in different states. Thus, before embarking on a discussion of the different ways to analyze artifacts, it would be prudent to clarify how the term *artifact* will be used in this book.

ARTIFACTS

I teach my students that *artifacts* are objects that are made or modified by humans. This seemingly straightforward definition can quickly become fatally vague if subjected to intense scrutiny. Is a building foundation an artifact? A trashpit? The unmodified rocks surrounding a hearth? A deer ulna found in a trashpit? Items made by *Homo erectus?* All of these items can appear on archaeological sites and aid in archaeological interpretation, but calling them all artifacts stretches the definition to the breaking point. Kenneth Feder (1996:458) offers a definition that clarifies the situation somewhat: "*artifact*—Any object manufactured by a human being or human ancestor, but usually a portable object like a stone spearpoint or a clay pot as distinguished from more complex archaeological features." This clears up some of the confusion, but what of unmodified portable objects?

ECOFACTS

Unmodified items that are found on and aid in the interpretation of an archaeological site are sometimes referred to as *ecofacts*. Actually, the only time you see this term is in texts such as this one. Still, the term is useful for those who split hairs, and it usually applies to the bulk of faunal and floral remains recovered at an archaeological site. For example, at an early nineteenth-century fur-trading post excavated in northwestern Wisconsin, I examined the faunal remains recovered from the site. Though these animal bones were not made by the inhabitants, an analysis of these remains determined the season of occupation for the site and the dietary preferences of the fur traders, and they even contributed to a determination of which cabin was occupied by the high-status company partner and which was used by the lower-status employees (Ewen 1986).

Animal bone and other objects, such as the individual rocks surrounding a hearth or pollen sealed in a trashpit, were associated with the site's inhabitants though technically not made by them. It is important to note that ecofacts are often subjected to the same analytical scrutiny by archaeologists as artifacts. Therefore, their analysis will be discussed at some length in this volume

Artifacts and ecofacts are the stuff of archaeological analysis. However, they all are meaningless if the context in which they were found was not recorded or later lost.

CONTEXT

Archaeological sites are like crime scenes of the past. Both archaeologists and detectives attempt to reconstruct past events from the physical remains of those events. It is important not only to collect the evidence but to record its precise location as well. This is why crime scenes are roped off from the public until the area has been minutely photographed and studied. In this way, archaeological sites are very much like crime scenes since the average visitor to a site is rarely permitted to jump in the pit with the excavators.

Knowing the context is what makes artifact analysis possible. Understanding where an artifact was found on a site and its relationship to other artifacts, ecofacts, and features is crucial for the archaeologist. I mentioned earlier that artifact analysis was the second most important factor separating the archaeologist from the pothunter. The concern for context is the most important factor that separates the archaeologist from the looter. It is an artifact's context that makes analysis possible by allowing you to determine its function and placement in time and space.

The importance of the archaeologist's obsessive concern with context is amply demonstrated by my excavations at the Governor Martin site in Tallahassee, Florida. Finds of sixteenth-century Spanish coins, ceramics, and beads led archaeologists to believe that they had located the site of Hernando de Soto's first winter encampment (ca. 1539–1540). However, the possibility that these materials could have been the result of the earlier (1528) expedition of Pánfilo de Narváez or salvaged and traded shipwreck material could not be dismissed. During the last month in the field for the project, the shattered jaw and several teeth from a domestic pig (*Sus scrofa*) were recovered from an undisturbed deposit in association with protohistoric Apalachee Indian pottery and a sixteenth-century Nueva Cadiz bead. The context of the pig teeth is important, because pigs are not native to the southeastern United States. Historical records indicate that de Soto, not Narváez, was the first to introduce pigs into the region. After de Soto passed through, Spaniards would not venture back into this part of Florida for another hundred years. Thus, without the sixteenth-century context established, the pig bones might have been evidence of just another southern barbecue.

As anthropologists, archaeologists are concerned with two types of context: the archaeological context and the cultural context. The cultural context is important in that, in addition to the description of human behavior and its consequences, it consists of the interplay of these actions and how they function within the larger cultural system. The archaeological context, on the other hand, *comes from* the material results of cultural behavior. It can be used to infer the lifeways characteristic of the former occupants of the site. It is from the archaeological context that we can infer the cultural context in which the artifacts were used.

RANGE OF MATERIAL INCLUDED

The range of artifacts that are analyzed and the scope of that analysis depend on several factors: the expertise of the archaeologist, the requirements of the scope of work (in the case of contracts or grants), and the funding available for the project. Often a bewildering array of material is found on an archaeological site, and there are few (if any) Renaissance individuals who are expert in them all. More often than not, an archaeologist chooses to become proficient in a certain category of artifacts, such as lithics or glass beads. Still others focus on a single time period and ethnicity, such as the artifacts of the Spanish Colonial period or Paleoindian period.

Ivor Noël Hume (1972:13–14) has stated, "The excavator whose experience is confined to English colonial sites will be out of his depth if he tries to interpret those of Spanish origin." Unfortunately, archaeologists employed in CRM-oriented archaeology usually do not have the luxury of specifying which types of sites they will excavate. Those choices are dictated by the contract and the personnel available at their company. The larger firms may be able to hire archaeologists who specialize in either historic or prehistoric archaeology, but circumstances often require these specialists to interpret types of sites outside their specialty. For this reason, it is usually a good idea to engage an appropriate specialist on a project when the variety of the artifact assemblage exceeds your ability to conduct a complete analysis.

The biggest challenge for many contract firms, in the realm of artifact analysis, is having the staff expertise to analyze the material recovered from both prehistoric and historic sites. This is because the latter requires additional research skills not always taught in the anthropology curricula to which most archaeologists are exposed. Until the latter half of this century, this was not a problem since virtually all archaeology (with a few notable exceptions) done in the United States was performed on prehistoric sites. Even as late as the 1970s, most contract archaeologists and the state historic preservation officers (SHPOs) to whom they reported paid little attention to historic sites, especially those dating to the nineteenth century and later. Though quite a bit of discussion still ensues about the significance of late historical archaeological remains (Ewen 1995; Cabak et al. 1999), today's cultural resource manager can no longer ignore them with impunity. Even twentieth-century tenant farmsteads and World War II military camps are now eligible for inclusion on the National Register of Historic Places and therefore *must* be taken into consideration by archaeological survey teams.

PREHISTORIC

Defining what is historic and what is prehistoric is not as straightforward as it may seem. In fact, this was no small matter of debate in the early days of historical archaeology. Obviously prehistoric sites are those occupied before written history. But what comprises a historic site? Even restricting this question to the Americas does not clear up all the ambiguity. If you answer, "It is a site that has historic documents associated with it," you eliminate many sites that were never documented in the historic record or whose documentation has been lost or destroyed. If you say (for the New World), "Any site dating after 1492," you are suggesting that a fifteenth-century Mississippian village in Illinois is prehistoric and that the same village a century later is historic even though the inhabitants, in both cases, never met a European and shared a similar material culture.

Is the question of whether a site is historic or prehistoric even meaningful? Of course it is. How an archaeologist classifies a site will often determine his or her approach to its analysis and interpretation. It determines the questions asked of the archaeological record and the expertise that is needed to interpret the site in question. Interpreting historic sites usually requires that the archaeologist possess the additional skills to conduct research in the documentary record or at least have a qualified historian on the research team.

Many prehistoric archaeologists feel that analyzing historic artifacts is easier to do since there are often documents describing their function, distribution, and sometimes even their price. Historical archaeologists counter that function and worth are unverifiable for prehistoric artifacts and that the analysis of historical artifacts is actually more challenging since the range of material is far greater and there is always the chance that a document will appear that refutes their initial interpretation! It is probably more prudent to say that each analysis of prehistoric and historic artifacts presents different challenges to an interpretation that must be overcome by the archaeologist in different ways.

3

ARTIFACTS AND ARCHAEOLOGICAL THEORY

Archaeology, like most disciplines, has changed its focus over time. The pace of these changes is similar to the punctuated equilibrium of evolutionary biology. There are periods during which the research questions of archaeologists follow relatively similar lines (i.e., reconstruction of past chronologies). These periods of little change are punctuated by scholarly upheavals, which some liken to paradigm shifts, where the focus of research takes a new direction. Needless to say, the reorienting of archaeological research results in an entirely new suite of questions being asked of the archaeological assemblage. It is interesting to note that it is the new research orientation that precedes the analytical technology rather than the other way around.

As the questions being asked of the artifacts change, the methods of analyses also change to accomplish these new goals. For example, a pot is recovered from a burial at a prehistoric site in the Plains. The methods of analyzing this artifact will change according to whether the archaeologist wants to know the age of the pot, whether the pot was locally made or a trade item, the function of the pot, or the gender of the individual who made it.

What factors influence archaeological interpretation? The prevailing social values at the time a site is analyzed often affect interpretation as does the training of the archaeologist. Not so long ago, most archaeologists looked to science to reveal the "truth" about the past. Today, many archaeologists see the past as a social construction with multiple, equally valid interpretations. Archaeologists needn't necessarily buck the trends in current archaeological research, but they should constantly question their validity. Being aware of the origins of research trends helps keep them in perspective and allows an assessment to be made of their potential to contribute to the long-term goals of the discipline. For this reason, it is often instructive not only to learn the different approaches utilized in archaeology but to understand something about the times in which they were conceived. The historical perspective permits the identification of subjective factors by observing how and, perhaps, why interpretations change through time.

Archaeological theory can be said to be hierarchically arranged with high, middle, and low levels (Trigger 1989:19–25). *Low theory* consists of observable, regular phenomena (e.g., typologies, seriation, dating) and does *not* refer to human behavior. *Middle theory* includes generalizations accounting for regularities between datasets or variables (e.g., population pressure and the development of agriculture). This level relates human behavior to archaeological data. *High theory* is what most students think of when they discuss archaeological theory. It can be equated with controlling models (paradigms) such as Marxism, cultural materialism, or processual archaeology. While all levels of theory have an effect on the type of analyses being performed, it is the highest level that influences all the others.

Does a discussion of archaeological theory have *any* relevance for the contract archaeologist who is surveying a right-of-way corridor for a proposed highway or a Forest Service archaeologist who is charged with managing the cultural resources of a national forest? Surprisingly, more than you might think, especially when interpreting artifacts or assessing site significance. If your goal is to reconstruct the past lifeways of a site's inhabitants, you are going to analyze the artifacts differently than if you were concerned with the processes affecting culture change or understanding how past belief systems were shaped by and reflected in a society's material culture. It is important to understand something of the history of archaeological reasoning in order to better interpret past site reports.

The history of archaeological thought can be reduced, in its most general sense, to three basic movements in which the many different approaches can be grouped: constructing culture history, processual archaeology, and postprocessual archaeology.

CULTURE HISTORY

The construction of local and regional culture histories has been, is, and will continue to be important to the field of archaeology. Essentially, this approach is characterized by descriptive work that deals with the who, what, where, when, and how of past societies and characterizes most of CRM archaeology today. It is the particularistic baseline data from which all inferences about the past are derived and tested. It is a necessary first step for all archaeology and one that many claim is still unfinished for most areas of the country. Indeed, the October 1999 issue of *North Carolina Archaeology* is devoted to "Prehistoric Pottery: Series and Sequence on the Carolina Coast" and explicitly follows "in the spirit of . . . Bill Haag's initial explorations" that established the original pottery seriation for the region (Herbert 1999:2).

PROCESSUAL

The New Archaeology was introduced in the late 1960s by archaeologists who thought that the basic regional temporal-spatial frameworks were well enough defined to start addressing questions concerning how and why cultures changed through time. This is an explicitly positivistic and nomothetic approach, which uses research design and the scientific method to analyze conditions of culture change and to generate laws governing human behavior.

Several approaches are subsumed under what has come to be known as *processual archaeology* (e.g., general systems theory, cultural ecology). *Processual* refers to the processes of culture change that take place as a result of interactions between a culture and its natural and cultural environment. This approach proved particularly well suited to many regional CRM and academic studies. The Cache River Basin Project (Schiffer and House 1975) and Deagan's (1983) study of colonial St. Augustine are good examples of processual archaeology.

Louis Binford, the leading exponent of the processual approach, concentrated on understanding culture change as an internal process, thus emphasizing the systemic aspects of culture. He differed from traditional archaeologists by focusing on the human ability to innovate while at the same time agreeing that cultures tended to remain static if undisturbed. He also agreed that human behavior was determined by forces (usually natural) of which humans were largely unaware.

Artifacts in an archaeological assemblage function in three subsystems of culture: technomic, sociotechnic, and ideotechnic. This type of approach has real repercussions when employed on artifact assemblages! Regularities in human behavior could be used to infer many aspects of prehistoric cultures that could not be directly correlated with the archaeological record. Binford denied the relevance of psychological factors and instead focused on identifying relations between technology and the environment as the key elements for determining cultural systems and, hence, human behavior (Trigger 1989:294–303). The apparent lack of concern for the impact of the individual led to the responses, which have come to be known collectively as the postprocessual school of thought.

POSTPROCESSUAL

Postprocessual archaeology subsumes theoretical approaches (largely apositivistic) that are critical of an allegedly unbiased scientific approach and that emphasize the individual and social factors in human societies. These include feminist, critical theory, and neo-Marxist approaches to archaeology. The extreme view of postprocessualism rejects the objectivity of the scientific approach and indeed whether the "truth" is really out there.

This relativistic stance claims that the interpretation of the past is dependent on the perspective of the observer or, in this case, archaeologist. Thus, multiple interpretations of the past are possible, all of which are equally valid. This is a disturbing thought for those trying to discover "what really happened." The implications for CRM-oriented archaeology are troubling, specifically with regard to the interpretation of site significance. On the other hand, the emphasis on the individual and disenfranchised groups has led to a great deal of archaeology concerning African slaves, Chinese immigrants, and other so-called people without history.

CULTURAL RESOURCE MANAGEMENT

In 1966, a bill was signed into law that marked the single most important change in archaeology as it is practiced in the United States. Section 106 of the National Historic Preservation Act states:

> The head of any Federal agency having direct or indirect jurisdiction over a proposed Federal or *federally assisted undertaking* [emphasis mine] in any State and the head of any Federal department or independent agency having authority to license any undertaking shall prior to

the approval of the expenditure of Federal funds on the undertaking or prior to the issuance of any license, as the case may be, take into account the effect of the undertaking on any district, site, building, structure, or object that is included in or eligible for inclusion in the National Register. The head of any such Federal agency shall afford the Advisory Council on Historic Preservation established under Title II of this Act a reasonable opportunity to comment with regard to such undertaking.

This legislation is so important because it means that any project that involves the federal government *in any way* might potentially require the services of an archaeologist. Section 106 catapulted archaeology from an obscure, romantic academic pursuit to a full-fledged environmental industry in less than a decade.

The National Historic Preservation Act was largely responsible for what has come to be known as cultural resource management (unless you work for the U.S. Forest Service, in which it is called heritage resource management). Cultural Resource Management (CRM) is simply archaeology performed under legal mandate and accounts for nearly 80 percent of all the archaeology done in the United States today. What does this have to do with artifact analysis? A great deal, actually, since state and federal guidelines regulating CRM archaeology often mandate what type and number of artifacts are to be collected and the types of special analyses required to satisfy an archaeological contract.

It is important for the archaeologist to know the guidelines of the agency or institution that is sponsoring or reviewing the archaeological project. For instance, artifacts collected on a project for the National Park Service must be inventoried according to their cataloging system (formerly the Automated National Catalog System, now Re:discovery). Similarly, other federal agencies and many state agencies have specified formats for cataloging and curating their data. It should be noted that there is no uniform standard across the United States. Archaeologists should contact the state archaeologist before pursuing a compliance project in their states to determine which procedures, if any, need to be followed.

This caveat does not necessarily mean that the data must be analyzed in a particular way. Rather, after the analyses are complete, the data must be left in a manner that is compatible with data from other projects sponsored by the particular agency. Ignorance of acceptable formats can result in much duplicated effort if the cataloging and reporting of the artifacts must be redone to conform to a specific agency's guidelines.

CONCLUSION

The remainder of this book will explore various methods and techniques of artifact analysis. It is not meant to be a step-by-step guide to the "right way" to analyze artifacts. There are many ways to analyze artifacts. The right way will depend on the questions being asked of the artifact assemblage. Often, archaeologists will quantify and organize artifacts in a specific way because "that's the way they learned it in grad school." The purpose of this volume is to expose the archaeologist to multiple systems of analysis and the rationale as to when they are appropriate.

The continuing theme of this volume will be the importance of relating your analytical methods to your research questions. All archaeological projects have (either explicitly or implicitly) a multistage research procedure. The stages include problem design, project implementation, data acquisition, data processing and analysis, interpretation, and publication (Fagan 1997:102–4; Hester et al. 1997:21–24). Each step refers back to the initial step: problem design. In many CRM archaeological projects, the questions to be answered are specified in the scope of work. Fieldwork, analysis, interpretation, and the production of the final goal should focus on answering those specific questions. Once they have been addressed, other questions can be considered, depending on the time and money available.

PART II

PREPARING FOR ANALYSIS

In this section, the focus is on the activities that allow the process of analysis to begin. Again, the importance of maintaining the context of the excavated artifact is paramount. Processing the artifacts is cleaning them to the extent that they can be described and identified and rough sorted into material categories. This expedites the cataloging process and identifies artifacts in need of special treatment.

Cataloging the artifact assemblage is the beginning of analysis. The goal here is twofold: (1) to inventory the collection and (2) to organize the collection to facilitate its interpretation by the archaeologist. Labeling of artifacts is a time-consuming but often necessary task for the archaeologist in the unending effort to preserve the provenience data associated with an artifact. The preservation of the artifact itself and stabilization procedures must be considered before the artifact is removed from the ground.

Finally, the use of digital imaging is discussed not only as a way of making a permanent record of the artifact that can be shared with colleagues across the country but also as a technique to enhance an artifact's attributes to aid in its analysis.

4

 **EXCAVATING ARTIFACTS**

Getting the artifacts out of the ground is the first phase of their odyssey from excavation to curation. What happens in the field and on the way to the lab is of vital concern to the archaeologist, for it is here that specimens are most likely to be lost or commingled, which will wreak havoc with the analysis and interpretation of the site. It is crucial to the success of a project to ensure that proper care is taken of the artifacts during this preanalysis phase.

The methods employed in the excavation of artifacts is beyond the scope of this volume and, indeed, is the subject of volume 3 in The Archaeologist's Toolkit. However, the excavation of artifacts does have a bearing on the analysis phase of the project. Obviously, the recovery techniques employed will determine what there is to analyze. For example, using water flotation techniques might result in the recovery of small animal bones and seeds, which might necessitate engaging a zooarchaeologist or ethnobotanist. Conversely, improper stabilization in the field of wet, friable wooden or bone artifacts might mean that these specimens do not survive to be analyzed.

RECORDING CONTEXT

As discussed earlier, the importance of context cannot be overemphasized. The artifact loses most of its interpretive value if the context in which it is found is lost. Therefore, it is crucial to record the provenience of artifacts as they are discovered. *Provenience* (or *provenance* if you are an art historian) refers to the three-dimensional location of the artifact in space. This is usually determined in the field by referencing the artifact's horizontal location using the site's grid system (x- and y- axes) and the vertical location (z-axis) in reference to an arbitrarily established datum plane or depth from ground surface (see Tooklit, volumes 2 and 3). The provenience can be recorded either for the particular artifact (as in the case of piece plotting) or for the archaeological deposit (e.g., level within an excavation unit, feature, surface find) in which the artifact is found.

Recording of the provenience in the field is important given the inherently destructive nature of archaeological excavation. Thus, the information recorded in the field forms the basis for all that follows in the lab. There are a number of ways that archaeologists record provenience. One common method is to establish a provenience catalog, often referred to as a field specimen (FS) catalog. The field specimen number is used in the field to designate provenience and is assigned to each level or group of artifacts for which specific provenience needs to be recorded. It is assigned sequentially for each provenience and is written on the bag in which the artifacts are put as well as recorded in the FS catalog. It is absolutely crucial, to the analysis phase of the project, that the information in the provenience catalog correspond to that on the bags of collected artifacts. This may sound laughably obvious, but on a large project that may generate hundreds of FS numbers and thousands of individual artifacts, mistakes are often made, requiring hours of backtracking in the lab.

COLLECTING

What archaeologists collect and what they discard will have a bearing on the analysis of the artifact assemblage. Every archaeologist must decide at the outset of a project what they will collect and what they will leave behind in the field. This may sound like an outrageous statement to the novice since obviously everything is important and must be collected. Unfortunately, this approach is usually not practical, though sometimes the data may be recovered even if the artifacts themselves are not. An example will help clarify this seemingly paradoxical statement.

Puerto Real is a sixteenth-century Spanish Colonial outpost on the northern coast of Haiti. Archaeological excavations at this site have concentrated on the public buildings on the main plaza and on commercial and residential structures nearby (Ewen 1991; Deagan 1995).

During the excavation, thousands of pieces of glass, metal, and ceramics were found. Also uncovered were literally tons of brick and stone used in the construction of the town. To ship back all the construction debris to the archaeological laboratory at the University of Florida was not practical. Yet, the data they represented concerning the location and architecture of the site were crucial. So that all the data were not lost, the bricks and stones were counted, weighed, and, where appropriate, measured. Thus, the important information was gathered without the expense of shipping back several thousand pounds of brick and stone. Representative samples of these materials were also collected should petrographic or other specialized analyses be desired in the future.

Obviously, some data categories lend themselves more than others to the kind of sampling discussed here. The question of discarding data is a difficult one for all scientists, not just archaeologists. You must always keep in the back of your mind that new techniques may be developed or new perspectives embraced that will make seemingly useless or redundant data valuable. Yet, there is the problem that you simply can't save everything. This is also a fiscal consideration for contract firms that must pay another agency to curate the artifacts recovered on their projects. The best compromise is to save what is important now and sample the rest.

Another problem for the archaeologist is how much attention must be paid to artifacts from components other than the one in which you are interested. Agatha Christie Mallowan (1946:40) discusses this dilemma, which she encountered while helping her archaeologist husband, Max Mallowan, survey for sites in Syria. "The mounds in the immediate neighbourhood of Meyadin prove unattractive. 'Roman!' murmurs Max disgustedly. It is his last word of contempt. Stifling any lingering feeling I may have that the Romans were an interesting people, I echo his tone, and say 'Roman,' and cast down a fragment of the despised pottery." Lady Mallowan might be forgiven for such an attitude since she was a volunteer on the project, but today's archaeologist cannot. It is important to take the same care with the artifacts in which you are not immediately interested as with those that you are. Someone will be interested in those data even if you are not.

A good example of the value of other components is the recent work at the Governor Martin site in Tallahassee, Florida (Ewen and Hann 1998). The focal component was associated with the first winter encampment of Hernando de Soto. However, to get to that component, it was necessary to dig through a World War II period officer's club, an antebellum plantation, a Seminole Indian village, and a seventeenth-century Spanish mission. Below the de Soto component was an earlier Apalachee Indian village, and the lowest level showed traces of an early Archaic occupation. Although the de Soto–related artifacts were of particular interest, the other components were not ignored as they both affected and were affected by the Spanish encampment. Subsequent publications (Ewen 1989, 1996; Ewen and Hann 1998) concentrated on the contact period component, but those artifacts not related to the de Soto expedition were processed and inventoried and await future research in the curation facility at the Bureau of Archaeological Research in Tallahassee.

5

 **PROCESSING**

The foundation of the analyses and interpretation to come is the maintenance of the context for the artifact assemblage. It has been said that archaeology differs from cultural anthropology in that we kill our informants! Since a site is destroyed by the process of excavation, it is imperative that the context be recorded for all data. This is because the site will literally be re-created on paper back in the laboratory. Old houses are often disassembled before moving and their components numbered so that they can be reassembled on a new site.

The same analogy applies to the data from an archaeological site. As computer capacities evolve, we may soon see virtual sites that can be reexcavated again and again. Indeed, this is already evident in the archaeology on the Fredricks site in North Carolina. The final report has been put on CD as *Excavating Occaneechi Town: Archaeology of an Eighteenth-Century Indian Village in North Carolina* (Davis et al. 1998). Utilizing the storage capacity of the compact disk, the user is very nearly able to re-create the dig and reanalyze the data recovered.

ARTIFACT CHECK-IN

When moving from the field to the lab, the primary goal is to ensure that all recovered artifacts and their field documentation (bag tags, field forms, notes, and photographs) are accounted for and that no discrepancies between the artifacts and their documentation exist. The easiest way to accomplish this is to arrange the artifact bags in order according to their FS number and check it against the FS catalog.

Some archaeological programs don't assign FS numbers in the field, preferring to arrange bags in a logical provenience order back in the lab (i.e., grouping all bags from the same excavation unit together) and then assigning FS numbers and producing a catalog. This practice is not recommended since bags could be lost in the field, and lab personnel would not see any discrepancy and so never realize the loss. Also, entering the catalog into a computerized database allows the investigator to sort the field specimens into any order desired based on a variety of criteria.

All of the field documentation should be duplicated and filed separately from the original documents. This provides a backup in case anything happens to the originals. It also allows the analyst to have a working copy of the field notes and maps. Scanning or manually entering these documents and images into a computerized database is becoming an increasingly popular way to archive field notes and photographs and provides a convenient way to access these data.

CLEANING

Washing artifacts is often the first exposure the student or interested layperson has to actually doing archaeology. This task is usually seen by the project director as something an untrained volunteer can do to assist the archaeologist without getting into too much trouble. While this is true up to a point, the lab assistant must beware of potential problems lest an artifact be damaged in the cleaning process. Invariably those artifacts most prone to damage are the most valuable to the interpretation of the site.

The purpose of cleaning artifacts is to remove soil or other debris that may obscure important attributes of the artifact. If all diagnostic attributes are visible or if cleaning the artifact would remove important information (e.g., cleaning a sixteenth-century copper coin may remove the faint markings on the surface that would identify it), then the artifact should be left as it was found pending consultation with a qualified conservator. Individuals involved with cleaning artifacts should always err on the side of caution and check with the lab manger or project director if they are unsure whether an artifact will withstand the cleaning procedure.

The basic tools for the artifact washer are inexpensive and readily available. They consist of a tray to empty the artifact bag into (an old cafeteria tray works well), a plastic washbasin for holding water, a variety of brushes of different sizes and stiffness (e.g., toothbrushes, nail brushes, and various paintbrushes), a drying rack, and a hand sieve. A number of other specialty brushes and picks might be suitable for removing dirt from the artifact, but they are merely variations on a theme and subject to individual preference.

The concern for context is especially important at the cleaning stage since artifacts are likely to be separated from their bags on which is written all the provenience information. One cannot be too paranoid in this situation. If the bag associated with the artifacts is lost or two bags from different proveniences are mixed, then valuable data are lost. So the first order of business is to check the provenience information on the artifact bag for completeness and to make sure that this information stays with the artifacts. Put the empty bag (or make a tag with the provenience information) into the section of the drying screen that you are using for the artifacts after they are washed.

Empty the contents of the artifact bag onto a tray so that you can see what you have before immersing the material in water. Many categories of artifact should not be put into the washbasin. Separate out plant remains such as nutshells, wood fragments, cane, even grass— do not waste time washing these obviously modern debris. Also do not wash metal objects, radiocarbon samples, bone, or any object that will degrade in water. Some prehistoric potsherds, burned clay, or daub tend to disintegrate if left too long in water. When in doubt, a gentle dry brushing is the safest course of action.

Some archaeologists prefer to do the initial soaking in warm soapy water followed by a clear water rinse. The superiority of soapy over clear water appears negligible, and one does run the risk of losing artifacts in the suds! Make sure that the artifact bag is empty before setting it aside.

Washing the artifacts is a delicate process. It is often a good idea to place glass (unless it is patinated and flaking) and historic ceramics in the water to soak. Brush them with a soft brush, making sure that all edges are clean. Do not scrub stone flakes or chipped lithic tools as you may want to conduct microscopic examination of some of these flakes and tools; vigorous scrubbing might alter their appearance. Clean these using finger pressure only. Never roughly brush prehistoric ceramics or clay objects as this may score their surfaces. Try to dry-clean them using a dry, soft brush. If this does not work, dip them quickly in water and rub with your fingertips only. Make sure the edges of all potsherds are clean so as to reveal their temper. Some prehistoric ceramics have slips applied to their surfaces that brush off

easily. This is also true of overglaze decorations on historic ceramics
(e.g., many Japanese porcelains or European ceramics have gilded ac-
cents that rub off easily). Just remember that the purpose is to reveal
attributes important for the analyses, not to have them clean enough
to eat from.

Over the years a variety of automatic washing systems have been
devised, and some archaeologists swear by them, though most swear
at them. These range from manually rotated cylinders that fit into
water tanks to wire racks that fit in modern dishwashers. Most of
these devices are meant for bulk cleaning of durable objects, and they
suffer from lack of control over individual items and can result in a
drastic increase in sherd count. A colleague had good success with his
dishwasher set on delicate until the soil from repeated loads of artifacts ruined the machine's internal workings.

The washed artifacts should be placed on a drying screen to dry. A
drying screen is a wooden or metal frame supporting nylon window
screen. A rack usually holds several of these screens and allows for
the free circulation of air to facilitate drying (see figure 5.1). The
empty bag should accompany the artifacts on the screen or else a tag
with the appropriate provenience information. Do not mix bags on a
drying screen! After a bag of artifacts is finished, pour the water from
the wash basin through a screen or hand sieve to recover all the tiny
artifacts. Refill the wash basin with fresh water for each new bag.

Figure 5.1   Cleaning and drying artifacts. (Photo by C. Ewen.)

ROUGH SORTING

Rough sorting, another task that a student or lab volunteer can undertake with minimal training, can be accomplished in conjunction with the washing process. The purpose of this step is to speed the processes of cataloging and analysis by initially grouping the disparate artifacts into easily discernable, general categories. All artifacts from a common provenience can be combined into these general categories and bagged separately within the general provenience bag. These general categories might include prehistoric pottery, prehistoric lithics, unmodified raw material (e.g., rock), animal bone (faunal material), plant remains (floral material), historic ceramics, glass, metal, and a miscellaneous category. Rough sorting gives the project archaeologist a general idea of the range of materials present and facilitates the refinement of the categories into types and the removal of samples for specialized analyses.

6

 CATALOGING

The goals of artifact cataloging are twofold: (1) to provide the archaeologist with a complete inventory of the artifacts present in the collection and (2) to facilitate the analytical goals of the archaeologist. These two goals are complementary, yet satisfying both is curiously difficult to achieve. This is because the goals of the registrar, who is interested in a general artifact inventory and comparability between collections, are often at odds with those of the project archaeologist, whose main interest is answering the specific questions of the project's research design. This explains why the profession has not adopted a universal artifact cataloging system.

A good example of these conflicting goals was my own experience with the Automated National Catalog System (ANCS), formerly the standard system used by the National Park Service archaeologists. The ANCS (rhymes with *angst*) consisted of rigid categories in an inflexible format. All archaeological work performed by and for the Park Service was required to use this system. I'm told that the Park Service collection managers loved it. However, many of the archaeologists contracted by the Park Service chafed under a system that allowed little flexibility in the classification of artifacts and was extremely cumbersome to use for basic analytical procedures. While I was at the Arkansas Archeological Survey, our archaeologists would first enter the artifacts into our DELOS database (a UNIX-based relational database) and then reenter the collection into ANCS after the analyses had been completed. Thus, rather than expediting the lab work, the ANCS merely added another step (which we were not allowed to charge for!). The Park Service has since switched to a new, more flexible database (discussed later).

A cataloging panacea will not be presented here. Instead, a variety of options will be presented and the merits and shortcomings of each discussed. Special emphasis will be placed on the computerization of cataloging procedures and some of the current options available to the archaeologist.

ACCESSIONING

Every institution that curates archaeological collections has (or should have) an accession catalog that numbers all the individual artifact collections in its care. An accession number, though, can mean different things to different institutions. In its broadest sense, an accession number is a way of identifying a particular collection of artifacts. This is different from a site number. A single site that has been excavated for several seasons might have several accession numbers assigned to it, each representing the artifact collection from an individual field season. Conversely, a survey project may have a single accession number, even though several sites were found during the fieldwork. So when archaeologists accession the artifacts from their latest dig, this simply refers to the process of adding the current artifact assemblage to their institution's curated collections in such a way that it can be retrieved again as a coherent group.

The assignment of an accession number is highly variable among and often within institutions. For example, a site that has been excavated for four seasons may have four different accession numbers, one for each field season. Or, especially if the field seasons were consecutive, there may be only one accession number for the combined collections. However, if that site had been tested in the 1950s and then later fully excavated in the 1980s, there may be two accession numbers, reflecting the two distinct periods of archaeological investigation at that site. Ideally, the institution should have a consistent and formal policy for accessioning collections.

There are a variety of ways to designate an accession number. East Carolina University utilizes the simplest system of all. Each collection is assigned a new number sequentially as it arrives in the laboratory. A popular variation on this simple theme is to begin the accession number with the year in which the collection was made. Thus, the third collection to enter the lab in 1998 would receive the accession number 98-3. This approach is a good way to solve the dilemma of how to split up collections from multiple field seasons. It is also vulnerable to the overhyped millennium bug problem that allegedly plagued many computer systems (i.e., how would you tell a collection made in 1902 from one acquired in 2002?).

The accession catalog (figure 6.1) is not simply a list of all the numbers that have been assigned to collections. It records this number and other pertinent information such as site name and official state num-

05/26/2000   ECU Phelps Archaeology Laboratory   Page   1
                             Master Accession Catalog

Acc#	Site#	Sitename	Provenience	Recorder	Date Rec.
0001	8FR52	ST. VINCENT FERRY	ST. VINCENT ISLAND, FL	PHELPS	04-30-70
0002	8FR54	ST. VINCENT POINT	ST. VINCENT ISLAND, FL	PHELPS	05-01-70
0003	8FR60	ST. VINCENT 1	ST. VINCENT ISLAND, FL	PHELPS	04-30-70
0004	8FR61	ST. VINCENT 2	ST. VINCENT ISLAND, FL	PHELPS	04-30-70
0005	8FR63	ST. VINCENT 4	ST. VINCENT ISLAND, FL	PHELPS	04-30-70
0006	8FR64	ST. VINCENT 5	ST. VINCENT ISLAND, FL	PHELPS	04-30-70
0007	8FR65	ST. VINCENT 6	ST. VINCENT ISLAND, FL	PHELPS	04-30-70
0008	8FR66	ST. VINCENT 7	ST. VINCENT ISLAND, FL	PHELPS	04-30-70
0009	8FR67	ST. VINCENT 8	ST. VINCENT ISLAND, FL	PHELPS	04-30-70
0010	8FR68	ST. VINCENT 9	ST. VINCENT ISLAND, FL	PHELPS	04-30-70
0011	8FR69	ST. VINCENT 10	ST. VINCENT ISLAND, FL	PHELPS	05-01-70
0012	8FR70	ST. VINCENT 11	ST. VINCENT ISLAND, FL	PHELPS	05-01-70
0013	8TA35	BORKLUND MOUND	TAYLOR CO, FL	BORKLUND	05-00-70
0014	8WA10	BIRD HAMMOCK, MOUND B	WAKULLA CO, FL	HOLLIMAN	05-00-70
0015	8WA30	BIRD HAMMOCK	WAKULLA CO, FL	PHELPS ET AL.	01-00-70
0016	8WA86		WAKULLA CO, FL USDI	PHELPS	04-00-70
0017	8WA90		WAKULLA CO, FL USDI	PHELPS	04-10-70
0018		LAKE MARION	SOUTH CAROLINA	UNKNOWN	05-00-70
0019		BUNN COLLECTION	ZEBULON, WAKE CO	BUNN	05-00-69
0020		PUEBLO III	CORONADO NATIONAL MONU	SUTTON	05-00-67
0021		CERAMIC COLLECTION	TOME PUEBLO, NM		
0022		CERAMIC COLLECTION	ACOMA PUEBLO, NM		
0023		CERAMIC COLLECTION	OAKRIDGE, ROATAN ISLAN	SWIFT	08-16-69
0024		CERAMIC COLLECTION	"PALACIO", TLAXCALA HI	GONZALO	05-00-70
0025	8FR51	SOUTHERN DUNES			
0026	8FR4				
0027	8FR5				
0028	8FR24				
0029		J.O. SISSION HOUSE	SELMA, AL		
0030		HAMMER MILL	SELMA, AL		
0031	8GU11		BLACK ISLAND, ST. JOE	STAPOR	03-26-70
0032		8SA9	ALONG BEACH WEST OF GI		
0033	8WA51				
0034	8WA30	W.I. COMPOUND	FLORIDA	BEUCE	00-00-69
0035	31BF24	WHALEN SITE	BEAUFORT CO	KERWHEL ET AL.	00-00-69
0036	31PM1	SEA VISTA	PAMLICO CO	PHELPS	09-26-70
0037	31PM1	SEA VISTA (BEACH)	PAMLICO CO	PHELPS	09-26-70
0038	31BF24	WHALEN SITE	BEAUFORT CO	PHELPS	09-26-70
0039		DOG ISLAND	FLORIDA	STAPOR	04-14-70
0040	8FR71	PARADISE POINT	USDI; S.V.N.W.R.	STAPOR	04-14-70
0041	31NS3	THOMAS COLLECTION	ROCKY MOUNT, NC	THOMAS	11-03-70
0042	31NS3A		ROCKY MOUNT, NC	PHELPS	11-14-70
0043	31NS3B		ROCKY MOUNT, NC	PHELPS	11-14-70
0044	31NS3C		ROCKY MOUNT, NC	PHELPS	11-14-70
0045	8FR72		FRANKLIN CO, FL	STAPOR	12-12-70

Figure 6.1   Accession catalog. (Courtesy of the ECU Archaeology Lab.)

ber (if assigned), site location (usually by county), site excavator, the date the collection was added to the record, and any other relevant comments. Many repositories formerly had this information in an old ledger, which made finding a specific collection difficult if all the researcher knew was that the site had been dug in Greene County in the sixties—especially if there were several thousand accession records to search through. Fortunately, most repositories have entered their accession catalogs into a computerized database or spreadsheet, which allows for quick searches on a variety of categories. So, if all you knew was that Indiana Jones had left his Egyptian artifacts in your repository a long time ago, a query on the "Excavator" field in your database would quickly reveal all the accession numbers for which Dr. Jones was the excavator. It would also provide other information associated with those collections.

INVENTORY

An *artifact inventory* or *catalog* is a list of the artifacts within a particular collection. The inventory can vary in complexity depending on the use to which it will be put and the level of analysis conducted on the artifacts. A basic inventory would have the identified artifacts from a site list by provenience. That is, the contents of each FS would be listed in order for the site. Sometimes the artifact inventory is further subdivided by material (e.g., ceramics, lithics, etc.) or site component (i.e., prehistoric vs. historic), but the provenience information is always linked to the artifact.

The artifact inventory is the foundation of the analysis phase of the archaeological investigation. The subsequent manipulation of these data relies on the identification and provenience information being recorded in a logical and consistent manner. A well-constructed inventory allows the archaeologist to concentrate on those artifacts that will most affect the interpretation of the site while still having access to the entire range of data recovered from the site. For example, let's say the excavation of a late Archaic site recovers twenty-six thousand pieces of fire-cracked rock, thirty thousand bits of chert debitage, and forty-eight identifiable stone tools. The archaeologist can pull the tools from the artifact bags for further specialized analyses while shelving the rest of the collection, secure in the knowledge that most of the useable data concerning density and distribution across the site is recorded and available in the inventory.

A more elaborate inventory would include more than just the identified artifact and its associated provenience information. A complete inventory listing of an artifact could include such specific attributes as the material of which the artifact is composed; its weight, its color, and any decoration; its length and width; its age; the functional category to which it belongs; and any other information deemed pertinent by the archaeologist. The categories included in the inventory and the level of detail are determined by the research design associated with the particular project, although the basic inventory of artifact and provenience information should be recorded in all cases. The expanded archaeological catalog will be discussed at more length later in part 3 of this volume.

LABELING

In most archaeological laboratories across the country, a great deal of a lab assistant's time is spent writing tiny numbers on the surface of artifacts. This is done so that the provenience of the artifact will not be lost even if that artifact falls behind the lab table and is found months later during the annual lab clean-up day. The numbers laboriously inscribed on even tiny fragments of artifacts, at the very least, include the accession number and FS number (figure 6.2). They often include much more data.

The method and placement of this information is often rigorously prescribed by the institution. For example, the Arkansas Archeological Survey (Barnes and Cande 1994:11) requires the following information to be recorded on the artifact: the accession year and number, the FS number, the laboratory serial number (identifies subdivisions of the collection meaningful to the investigator), and the analytical serial number (identifies unique classes of artifacts such as rough sort categories, material/functional classes, or other analytical identifications). The number is applied with a drafting pen (formerly India ink on fine pen nibs was used) directly onto the surface of the artifact. If the artifact is dark colored, then white ink is used (a base coat of white correction fluid on which the number is written in black is a popular alternative at many institutions). Pieces of historic ceramics and glass are labeled on the edges, and prehistoric sherds are to be labeled on interior, undecorated surfaces. A clear coating of polyvinyl acetate, or PVA (clear nail polish is an economical alternative), is used to secure the ink on very smooth surfaces. Very small,

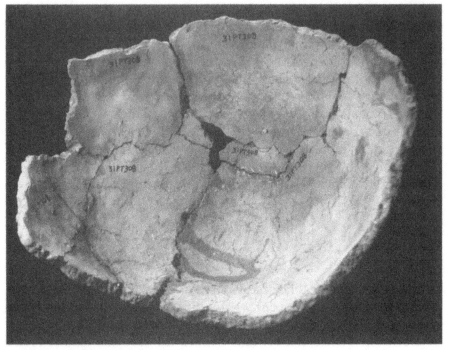

Figure 6.2   Numbered artifact. (Photo by C. Ewen.)

fragile artifacts or large numbers of small artifacts are allowed to have a tag with this information slipped in the bag with the artifact.

Not everyone agrees with this time-honored approach, and other concerns have tempered the zeal with which numbers are applied to artifacts. Though the paranoia over context is still very much in evidence, specialized analyses that retrieve information from the surface of artifacts (protein residue, AMS dating of soot, etc.) have caused some (see Sutton and Arkush 1998:28) to suggest that alternative methods of labeling be pursued. Also, the cost of this labor-intensive work is prohibitive for many small labs or private contractors.

A compromise that the author advocates is to label the bag containing the artifact(s) with an interior tag as well as writing on the bag itself. It is important to include an interior tag since the writing on the exterior of the bag tends to degrade over time. The artifact would only be physically labeled should it be separated from its bag for analytical (e.g., cross-mending) or display purposes.

7

 **FURTHER PREPARATION**

A number of other tasks are often necessary before the analysis of the artifacts can begin. Like cleaning and cataloging, they prepare the artifact so that the important attributes are readily observable or stabilized so as to survive analysis. Some of these tasks can be performed by the nonarchaeologist with minimal training.

RECONSTRUCTION AND CROSS-MENDING

A situation where labeling of individual artifacts is important is in the reconstruction or refitting of a whole artifact from its constituent pieces. The reconstruction of ceramic vessels is a common example of this practice, though any broken artifact can be reassembled if most of the pieces are present and the lab technician possesses enough patience. The importance of labeling is apparent if the constituent pieces of an artifact come from different proveniences.

Cross-mending is an analytical tool that allows the archaeologist to determine which proveniences are linked together. If an archaeologist has differentiated three strata on a site and they all contain pieces of the same pot, then it is likely that they are contemporary (barring disturbances that drag artifacts between levels). Having sherds with the same design or other attributes is not as telling as being able to physically link pieces from the same pot.

Reassembling the artifact also presents a better indication of the original item's form. For example, a shallow bowl and brimmed plate may have similar rim shapes. However, the reassembling of the body sherds with the rim fragments gives the analyst the vessel's true shape.

Reconstructing artifacts is one of the more popular lab activities in archaeology. There is something about the puzzle solver in most people that draws them to this task. It is one of the few activities that many lab technicians will pursue on their own time! Artifact reconstruction is delicate, tedious work often involving many hours to reassemble a single, highly fragmented vessel.

One of the strictest caveats in artifact reconstruction is reversibility. The technique that is used to reassemble the pieces should be reversible and not alter the original state of the fragments. That way, should it be discovered that the pieces were misassembled or need to be returned to their original provenience, then the artifact can be disassembled without damaging the individual fragments.

The usual procedure is to put the artifact back together two pieces at a time. First, two corresponding pieces are fit together and held with an adhesive such as water-soluble white glue or an acetone-soluble glue such as Duco cement. If the refit is truly temporary, masking tape can be used. The two joined pieces are then set in a sandbox to hold them in place until the adhesive sets. This procedure is repeated until the vessel is complete or all the available pieces are joined. Missing pieces can be filled with plaster or other suitable filler or simply left open (figure 7.1).

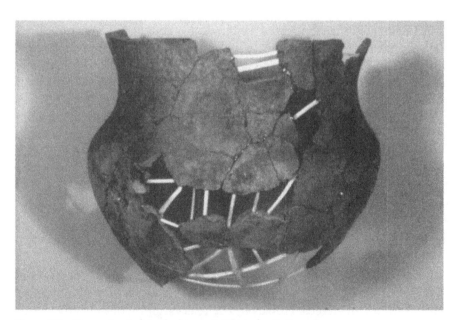

Figure 7.1   Reconstructed Apalachee pot. (Photo by C. Ewen.)

CONSERVATION

The stabilization and conservation of artifacts are important parts of the archaeological project. A complete discussion of artifact conservation is beyond the scope of this volume and is handled in more depth in another volume in this series (Toolkit, volume 6). However, a few comments here are appropriate. Artifacts made out of certain materials, such as iron, start to decay the moment they are put in a new environment (i.e., being deposited in the ground). Eventually they reach a state of equilibrium with this new environment, and corrosion slows considerably. The excavation of this artifact puts it back into another environment, which starts the decay process all over again. Plunging an artifact of this nature into a cleaning solution often further exacerbates the problem.

During the initial processing phase of a project, it is important to note which artifacts need conservation. If possible, these artifacts should be immediately sent to a conservator to stem the inexorable march of corrosion and decay. Unfortunately, that is not always possible due to funding constraints or the availability of a conservation facility and qualified personnel. In this case, steps should be taken to stabilize the artifact and the specimen flagged for conservation in the artifact catalog. The artifact should be sketched and photographed so that its original appearance is recorded in case the artifact suffers significant decay before conservation measures can be implemented.

Although it is best to have an on-site, or at least an on-staff, conservator/curator, such a position is often beyond the budget of most contract firms and small college labs. In this case, the project archaeologist will have to perform artifact first aid until the material can be sent to a specialist. Some practical advice can be founds in *A Conservation Manual for the Field Archaeologist* (Sease 1994), chapter 7 of *Field Methods in Archaeology* (Hester et al. 1997:143–58), and chapter 11 of *A Complete Manual of Field Archaeology* (Joukowsky 1980:244–75). Other useful sources include Dowman (1970), Hodges (1987), and Leigh (1978).

PHOTOGRAPHY

Photography is another useful technique in the archaeologist's toolkit and also the subject of a separate volume (Toolkit, volume 7). The proper depiction of an artifact in a report is literally worth a thousand lines of text in the final report involving some artifacts. However, there are some other good uses to which various imaging techniques can be applied during the early processing and analysis phases of an archaeological project.

CONVENTIONAL

As mentioned earlier, it is often a good idea to photograph an artifact before attempting conservation or any potentially destructive specialized analysis. The image of the artifact may be all that is left to the archaeologist to analyze if the original is somehow damaged or lost. It also saves handling and wear on the original, possibly delicate artifact (e.g., a corroded, sixteenth-century copper coin) if a photograph can be referenced rather than constantly exposing the fragile artifact to an unstable atmosphere.

Photographic techniques can also be used to enhance faint markings or decorations on an artifact, thereby aiding in its identification and interpretation. For example, the distinguishing marks on a copper coin recovered from the Governor Martin site (Ewen and Hann 1998:81) were barely legible, even when examined with a hand lens. By using oblique lighting and special film, it was possible to reveal enough detail in a photograph to identify the coin as a Spanish four-maravedi piece dating between 1505 and 1517. This helped link the site to the 1539–1540 winter encampment of Hernando de Soto.

Another type of conventional photography for analytical use is X-ray imaging. This technique often allows the archaeologist to peek beneath the corrosion to determine the nature of the artifact and assess its stability. Again, at the Governor Martin site, a rusted mass was X-rayed to reveal fourteen interconnected links, thus verifying the archaeologists' suspicions that the many separate iron rings previously found were actually bits of chain mail armor (Ewen and Hann 1998:78–79).

DIGITAL

The advent of affordable digital imaging devices and graphic manipulation software has already had a tremendous impact on the analysis of artifacts. I will try to avoid hardware- and software-specific discussions here since they will no doubt be outdated before this volume is published. The concepts involved, however, are valid, and the techniques discussed here will only be enhanced and made even more affordable as time passes.

Digital imaging simply refers to putting images (photographs, drawings, maps, etc.) into an electronic format so that they can viewed and stored on a computer. A conventional line drawing can be converted to a digital image by the use of a scanner or digitizing tablet. There are also digital cameras, which transfer images directly to a computer. These hardware devices have become increasingly affordable and are well within the budget of even the smallest archaeological laboratory. Video camcorders can also be connected to a computer equipped with a video capture board, and still images or entire movies can be saved in a digital format.

Once in the computer, digital images can be viewed and manipulated through various image-editing and -enhancing programs and computer-assisted drafting and design (CADD) software. Photographic enhancement software, such as Adobe's Photoshop, can be of great utility during the analysis phase of an investigation. Images can be enlarged, cropped, rotated, and inverted. To bring out obscured details, a photograph can be lightened or darkened, the contrast heightened, and negative images can be made positive. As with the conventional photographic techniques discussed earlier, it is often possible to extract details from an enhanced digital image that are not readily visible to the naked eye.

It is also possible to take a series of pictures of an artifact and then connect these into a single file. The image can then be rotated 360 degrees on screen to reveal all its sides. This technique is especially useful for fragile or unstable artifacts on which constant handling might damage the original specimen. This same effect can be achieved with a conventional camcorder and many repositories have made use of these technologies to record artifacts in their collections. This preserves at least some of the data should the artifact be repatriated or lost or damaged while on display.

Photographic images can also be converted to line drawings or color slides to black-and-white prints or negative images to positive. This is useful when a regular photograph has colors or shadows that obscure or overwhelm the more subtle attributes of an artifact. A good example would be the depiction of a chipped lithic artifact such as a projectile point. Archaeologists often prefer to portray these artifacts as line drawings since this method highlights fracture patterns and chipping techniques. The computer will render the surface treatment faithfully for examination, compensating for any lack of artistic talent on the part of the analyst.

Computer-assisted design programs, such as many CADD or metrical programs, have also been pressed into service by the artifact analyst.

Coupled with metrical software, it is possible to figure all the measurements of an object, including area and volume, if just one measurement is known. For example, the length of a potsherd is measured on the actual artifact, and then this dimension is indicated on an image of the artifact. The computer can now perform, with great accuracy, any other measurement desired of that artifact. More impressively, the computer can often use the measurements of the artifact fragment to extrapolate the size and shape of the original, intact specimen. For those interested in questions regarding vessel morphology, this is obviously a powerful tool.

Another use of digital imaging is the ability to store and retrieve pictures relating to all phases of an archaeological project. Thus, rather than holding multiple sheets of slides to the light or leafing through stacks of photographs to find a desired shot, the analyst can simply call up the image on a computer screen. Several computer applications allow an image to be stored along with descriptive data pertinent to that image. In essence, all the information from the field and lab photo log (photographer, date, subject, direction of the shot, provenience, and extensive commentary) can be linked to the image. By performing a query on the proper field(s), the archaeological analyst can quickly retrieve the plan view shot of a particular feature in a particular excavation unit. This image can then be printed or manipulated as necessary.

A couple of words of caution are in order regarding the use of digital imaging. First, though the cost of the hardware is coming down, the archaeologist must be aware of hidden or ancillary expenses. Using any graphics program and saving the images generated by them requires a substantial amount of computer memory, in terms of both desktop RAM and storage capacity. A single, high-density image can require well over a megabyte of space; a short video clip is usually well over a hundred megabytes. Most programs require a large amount of desktop RAM to run the graphics applications and a very large storage medium to store the images.

It would be foolish to offer advice on particular media when the technology is changing so rapidly. Not long ago a computer with four megabytes of RAM and a twenty-megabyte hard disk was sufficient for most applications. Today this doesn't even run most games! Removable storage media (e.g., tape drives, media cartridges, compact disks, and digital video disks) are evolving rapidly and offer a variety of storage solutions. It is probably prudent that these devices be purchased as external units, rather than built in, so that they can be upgraded as necessary.

PART III

ANALYSIS

Giving advice on artifact analysis to an archaeologist is a bit like telling a pitcher how to throw a baseball. How you accomplish the feat depends on what you want to do. To discuss all the intricacies of analysis of the myriad classes of artifacts is far beyond the scope of this volume. Key references devoted to the analysis of different types of artifacts are given wherever possible. Chapters 8 through 10 give a few examples of measurements and descriptions expected of artifacts in many contract reports. Chapter 11 suggests ways in which the archaeologist can organize the material assemblage from a site. Some advice and cautions are in order when using a computer to organize an archaeological database. Chapter 12 discusses how archaeologists have statistically manipulated their data to answer questions concerning pattern recognition, chronology, and spatial organization.

Part 3 wraps up with an all-too-often-ignored part of the analytical process: what to do with the artifacts after your immediate questions are answered. Others (or even you) may want to reanalyze the data at some point; how it is curated will determine how successful the reanalysis will be.

8

MATERIALS ANALYSIS

When asked to define artifact analysis, a graduate class in laboratory methods was initially nonplused. There was a great deal of confusion as to what actually constituted analysis. Some considered artifact identification and quantification to be analysis; others thought that it included the organization and interpretation of the data. One student finally opined that it was what the archaeologist did with the artifacts after they were excavated but before they were curated. In a sense, they were all correct.

David Hurst Thomas, in the third edition of his encyclopedic *Archaeology*, does not specifically define *artifact analysis*. Consulting the index, you are directed to a section concerning artifact dating. Another popular text refers to the sorting of artifacts into compositional categories and considering "the characteristics that differentiate one kind of data from others to show the ways that each can contribute to an understanding of past behavior" (Ashmore and Sharer 1996:114). Brian Fagan (1997:465), the author of many archaeological texts, simply defines *analysis* as "a stage of archaeological research that involves describing and classifying artifactual and nonartifactual data."

The actual analysis of the artifacts recovered from an archaeological project begins before the initial processing is complete. *Analysis* is defined by Webster's as a breaking up of a whole into its parts to find out their nature. In the case of archaeological analysis, an archaeologist separates the artifact assemblage into smaller categories in order to discern the nature of that assemblage. To what time period(s) does it date? What was its function(s)? Were the artifacts made locally, or did they come from some other place? How did the assemblage change through time? What does the assemblage say about the past culture's ideology? The first step toward answering these questions is the organization of the total assemblage into subsets that can shed light on these and other questions.

It would be wonderful if there were a single "right" way to organize the artifacts from an archaeological project. There would be a single text for the profession on which everyone would agree. Professors could drill their students with rote memorization until they got it right. Everyone's data would be compatible, allowing each archaeological culture to be described and fit into an "Archaeological Great Chain of Being." Unfortunately (or fortunately, depending on your perspective), this is not the case. This unrealistic view of "I love your database, and you love mine" only works if everyone is working in the same paradigm, asking the same questions and content with standardized data categories.

The last time there is very much agreement on archaeological classification is during the rough sorting stage. Here the artifact assemblage is broken down into the most basic category: material. Grouping artifacts on the basis of their composition is not only easily done by even the most untutored lab technician, but it is also a useful first step in the analytic process since many specific analytical techniques and conservation treatments depend on the artifact's composition. The basic material classes for prehistoric artifacts, discussed here, will include lithics, ceramics, metal, glass, and organic. These categories will be further subdivided chronologically into historic and prehistoric artifacts when appropriate.

LITHICS

Lithics refers to artifacts made out of stone. Sticklers for the English language would argue that archaeologists use the word improperly. It should be used as an adjective, as in "lithic artifacts," whereas most archaeologists use the term as a noun referring to the stone artifact subassemblage from their site as "lithics." You could argue the semantics if you could find someone who cared to, but modified (and unmodified) stones on a site are referred to as lithics by most archaeologists, so that is how the term is used here.

Stone artifacts are common on most archaeological sites because they are among the most durable of artifacts. The fact of their ubiquity and the fact that sometimes they are the *only* class of artifacts found on a site (e.g., lithic scatters make up the bulk of recorded sites in the offices of many state archaeologists) have caused many in the profession to claim that our view of the past is biased, and we might have termed the Stone Age the Basketry Age or Wood Age if preservation conditions on sites had been better. This may be, but since archaeologists are often limited to interpreting a site on the basis of a handful of stone flakes, a great deal of effort has been expended on the interpretation of lithic artifacts.

Though they may only represent a fraction of the total artifact assemblage that once existed at a site, lithics can tell us about many aspects of past life at those sites. The type of rock used to make the artifacts is indicative of the size of the site's catchment area, or it can be evidence of trade with other areas. How stone tools were made can reveal cultural affiliation or time period of manufacture. For example, a projectile point with a flute or channel flake removed longitudinally from its base is a good indication that it was made during the Paleoindian period (ca. 10,000 B.P.). The types of stone tools found in the artifact assemblage not only date that site but can provide the archaeologist with an idea of the site's function as well (e.g., raw material procurement, hunting, tool production, etc.). The type of analysis done on the lithic assemblage will depend not only on the questions asked but also on the kind of lithics present.

Unlike ceramics or most other artifact categories, which are formed by combining or adding material, stone artifacts are made by removing portions from the parent material. The study of this reduction process is the starting point for lithic analysis (see Carr 1994; Collins 1975; Crabtree 1972). In fact, the basic lithic category is nearly always broken down further into two categories, depending on the method of lithic reduction: ground stone or flaked stone.

It should be noted that the separation of the lithic artifacts into flaked or ground stone categories usually refers to the predominant mode of reduction on the finished artifact. A stone bowl would be classified as ground stone, even though its rough shape was pecked out, whereas an arrowhead would be classified with the chipped lithics even though the base was ground, presumably to dull the edges to permit hafting. To further muddy the classificatory waters, some types of stone, such as soapstone and catlinite, were actually carved before being polished into their final form. These are usually classified in an "Other Lithics" category or with the ground stone artifacts.

FLAKED/CHIPPED STONE

Flaked or chipped lithics are the result of the removal of stone fragments or flakes from a rock core. Most often this is accomplished by pressure or percussion being applied to the outside surface of a rock, although sometimes the heating of a rock can cause the pieces to pop off (a process known as *potlidding*). Typically, chipped lithics are made of stone that flakes in a predictable way such as flint (a type of chert), quartz, rhyolite, or a volcanic glass such as obsidian. Some types of stone are easier to work than others. The more predictable the breakage pattern, the easier the stone is to work. Obsidian and fine-grained cherts (such as from the Mill Creek formation in Tennessee) are considered easy to work and were highly sought throughout prehistory. Other kinds of raw material such as silicified sandstone or quartzite required more effort, yet they were used in the absence of more workable but less available material. It is important to know the geology of the area surrounding the site so that an assessment can be made as to where the material for the tools found at the site was from.

Humans have removed flakes from these materials by applying pressure or striking their surface either directly or indirectly. *Direct percussion* means simply striking the core or parent rock with another hard object (e.g., stone, bone, or antler). Sometimes the rock is rested on an anvil before striking, resulting in the method called *bipolar reduction*. *Indirect percussion* is accomplished by interposing another material, such as antler, to serve as a punch between the core and the hammerstone. The hammerstone strikes the punch, which indirectly transfers percussive force, thus striking off flakes. Another method of flake removal is the application of pressure. *Pressure flaking* is, as the name implies, the removal of flakes by the application of steady pressure rather than percussive force on an exposed edge. The result of either of these actions is a conchoidal fracture (shell-like flakes such as that inflicted on your windshield by a stone kicked up by the truck in front of you). Skillful placement of these conchoidal fractures removes flakes from a cobble and results in the production of a keen-edged stone tool such as a projectile point or a hide scraper that can, depending on the type of stone used, be sharper than surgical steel.

The analysis of the chipped lithic subassemblage is the subject of a great deal of diverse archaeological thought (Henry and Odell 1989; Flenniken 1984; Shott 1994). As is emphasized throughout this volume, the questions asked by the archaeologist will guide the type of analytical procedures performed. We can make some basic observations, however, that are common to many analytic approaches.

Besides noting the type of stone, it is usually important to indicate from which part of the stone the fragments derive. This means noting whether the flake has any cortex (unmodified exterior rock surface) and how much cortex is present. Primary decortication flakes have the majority of their surface consisting of cortex. Secondary decortication flakes have less cortex visible. Tertiary or thinning flakes have little or no cortex on their surface. The importance of this observation is that the proportions of the various types of flakes found at a site can indicate the stage of lithic reduction taking place. A site with a high proportion of primary decortication flakes might indicate quarrying activity with preliminary tool preparation. A lithic assemblage with a high proportion of thinning flakes would indicate tool finishing and reshaping activities.

Another qualitative observation that can be made is whether the artifact has been heat treated. It was discovered long ago, no doubt by some Paleolithic genius, that the workability of some stone types could be improved by subjecting it to intense heat (i.e., placing the cobble in a cooking fire). The reasons for this are not fully understood (see Domanski and Webb 1992; Flenniken and Garrison 1975), but the results are undeniable. Many types of stone fracture in a more predictable fashion after they have undergone heat treatment. Heat-treated stone can be recognized by a slightly pinkish color and a waxy feel to the surface.

The flake is a basic unit of analysis in lithic analysis. The landmarks on a flake consist of the striking platform, bulb of percussion, eraillure scar, and compression rings. As mentioned previously, an abundance of thinning flakes in the lithic assemblage is suggestive of tool manufacture. However, flakes can often be tools themselves. The context in which the flake is found and the presence of secondary retouching or microwear (i.e., polish) on its working edge can indicate the use of the flake as a tool.

Tools are the main concern of lithic analysis. Two general descriptive categories are bifaces and unifaces. The difference between them lies in how the working edge is achieved. *Bifacial* tools have flakes taken from both sides of the margin (the working edge), while *unifacial tools* have flakes removed from only one side of the margin. Bifacial tools include arrowheads and other projectile points, axes, cleavers, drills, and a host of other cutting or piercing tools. Unifacial tools are more restricted in their functions, serving primarily as hide-scraping and wood-shaving tools, though they were no doubt put to other uses as well. An example of a classic unifacial tool is an end scraper. Flake tools tend to be unifacial as well.

Cores are what remain of a rock or cobble after the useful flakes have been removed. Think of it as an apple from which successive bites have been taken until all the edible fruit has been consumed. However, the removal of the flakes does not necessarily end a core's use life. Often cores are converted into hammerstones as is evidenced by battering on one end. Sometimes a core will have one of its edges retouched (small flakes removed, usually by pressure flaking), suggesting that it had been pressed into service as a crude tool. This is especially likely in areas where good stone is scarce.

Analysis of chipped lithic artifacts can be as detailed as the archaeologist wants to make it. Measurements can be made of every conceivable dimension if the analyst has the time and money and the reason for doing so. However, there are some measurements that are routinely performed during analysis. The standard measurements (usually in millimeters) of lithic tools include length, width, and thickness; these should always be taken. Additional information for projectile points would include measurement of the various dimensions of the base (basal width, neck width, size and shape of notching) since the base is the most temporally and regionally diagnostic aspect of the projectile point (figure 8.1). The weight of the artifact is usually recorded (in grams) as well. Other questions concerning tool use and manufacture may require additional measurements. Consulting a lithic specialist or publications specifically relating to those kinds of questions would be necessary in those cases.

Debitage or stone waste flakes, another category of lithic artifacts, has received more attention recently (see Sullivan and Rozen 1985). It refers to the by-product of stone tool production. It includes flakes (discussed earlier), shatter (angular stone debris), and sometimes exhausted cores. A quick way to analyze your debitage from a site is to size grade the assemblage using nested screens of different size mesh (see Shott 1994 for a discussion of size grading). The size-sorted debitage can then be counted and weighed and other observations (e.g., type of stone, amount of cortex present, heat treatment) can be made for each size category. These data can be helpful in identifying activity areas and the activities within those areas at a site.

Most of the analytic techniques discussed here can be performed by the average archaeologist or lab technician. Some advanced techniques, however, will require the assistance of a lithic specialist.

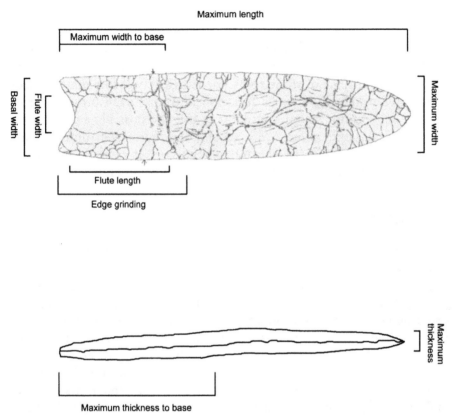

Maximum length

Maximum width to base

Basal width

Flute width

Maximum width

Flute length

Edge grinding

Maximum thickness

Maximum thickness to base

Figure 8.1   Attributes of projectile points. (Drawing by I. Randolph Daniel.)

Use-wear analysis has been conducted to help determine the function of various stone tools. Here, the edge of an archaeological specimen is examined under a microscope and compared to experimentally
prepared specimens that have been used for specific tasks (e.g., wood
working, hide scraping, butchering, etc.). The utility of this type of
analysis has been questioned given the multipurpose nature of many
stone tools as well as any postdepositional damage the artifact may
have suffered. Still, the results of use-wear analysis can be useful and
inspire questions that might otherwise not be considered (Vaughn
1985). For example, a site might have little in the way of faunal remains due to poor preservation in highly acidic soil. However,
the presence of stone tools exhibiting wear characteristic of bone
butchering might be the only indication that such activity occurred
at the site.

Residue analysis is a recent development that may cause archaeologists to never wash another rock! It is possible through such techniques as PIXE (proton-induced X-ray emission) analysis or the use of SEM (scanning electron microscopy) to identify materials adhering to the working surface of stone tools. Identification of this material can conclusively identify a tool's function and may even provide information concerning the environment of use and possibly a date (if the material is organic) using AMS (accelerated mass spectrometry) dating (Loy 1990). Like many specialized analyses, it can be challenging to find a lab that performs them and they are usually fairly expensive.

GROUND STONE

Ground stone artifacts are different from flaked stone artifacts in that grinding or polishing is the method of reduction rather than flaking. Often the grinding is preceded by a percussive pecking or even flaking to rough out the initial form. Granite, basalt, greenstone, and other igneous or metamorphic rocks lend themselves most readily to this method of reduction, although some of the more durable sedimentary rocks, such as limestone, lend themselves to ground stone tool making. Often the grinding that resulted in the final form of an artifact was a result of use, such as in the case of a mano (handstone) and metate (grinding platform). These tools may have originally been pecked into a rough shape, but it was years of grinding seeds that resulted in the final shape of the artifacts. Other artifacts were purposely ground and polished to their final shape, such as a chunkey stone (figure 8.2) or discoidal (a stone disk that was rolled down a court in a Native American game). Ground stone items such as monolithic axes (hafted axes manufactured from a single piece of stone), banner stones (atlatl weights), and gorgets (ornaments worn around the throat) are often interpreted as indicators of high status due to the large amount of time and effort invested in their manufacture.

When conducting an analysis of ground stone objects, archaeologists often can separate them into two basic functional categories: ornamental/personal and utilitarian. Examples of items placed in the ornamental/personal category might include gorgets, maces/batons, beads, and figurines. The latter group would include milling stones, bowls and other vessels, banner stones, various types of weights, and axe heads. Even with this simple division there are some judgment calls to be made as utilitarian items can be highly ornamented (e.g.,

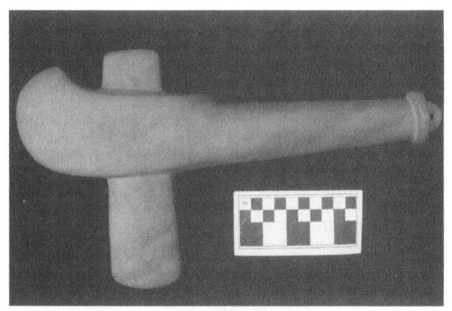

Figure 8.2 Monolithic ground stone ax. (Photo by C. Ewen.)

animal effigy plummets and banner stones), while other objects, such as gaming stones and pallets, could arguably fit into either category. This is but a glimpse of the artifact classification conundrum to be discussed later.

If one abandons a functional classification scheme, then description becomes paramount. In the case of ground stone objects, their basic form and material should be described so that someone who has never seen the item can visualize it properly. Measurements, as with flaked stone tools, should include length, width, and thickness as well as other dimensions deemed appropriate by the analyst. In the case of milling stones, depth of the concavity in the milling surface is usually measured. This is a good indication of relative duration of use when compared to other milling stones of similar material. A somewhat more difficult description concerns the method of manufacture. This involves a close examination of the surface of the stone to determine the direction of the striations (scratched lines left by the grinding process) and whether any intentional polishing (rubbing of the surface with another fine-grained substance) has taken place.

Advanced procedures such as residue analysis are also possible for ground stone tools. This is especially important for grinding stones since it should not be assumed that only corn or other types of seeds were being processed by these tools. Even if this were the case, it would be helpful to know the variety of seeds being ground. This kind of examination can be as simple as an inspection of the mill stone's surface with a hand lens for macroflora or other identifiable residue. Sophisticated techniques such as PIXE analysis are also possible with the same caveats as discussed with flake tools.

The analysis of stone tools is a basic task performed in an archaeological lab. Tools required include, at a minimum, a pan balance or electronic scale, a sliding caliper, a metric tape measure, a hand lens, and a Munsell color chart (for description of the color of the lithics). The procedures outlined earlier should be regarded as basic guidelines for the lithic analyst. A more in-depth treatment of lithic analysis can be found in chapters 4 and 5 of *Archaeological Laboratory Methods: An Introduction* (Sutton and Arkush 1998) and the various references cited previosuly.

CERAMICS

The term *ceramics* describes any item that is made of fired clay. Thus, the ceramics category can contain tea cups, chamber pots, roof tiles and the hardened exterior fragments of a wattle and daub structure that burned in antiquity. Ceramics are nearly as durable as stone and usually comprise the largest category of artifacts on sites postdating the domestication of plants, with which they are usually associated.

Because ceramics are ubiquitous on post–Archaic period sites, archaeologists try to squeeze the most data possible from them. Ceramics, for their part, are very obliging and can yield information pertaining to past foodways, the status of individuals with which they were associated, the cultural geography of a region, and they reveal trade patterns with other regions. They serve as good chronological tools and indicators of the technological prowess of their makers. Archaeologists have even used ceramics to gain insights into the belief systems and cognitive processes (e.g., Deetz 1996) of past cultures. As with every category of artifacts we will examine, the type of analysis performed on any ceramic assemblage will depend on the questions being asked.

One way of identifying the types of questions that ceramics can answer is to divide them on the basis of whether or not their primary function is food related. Food-related ceramics pertain to vessels used for storage (utilitarian wares), preparation (cooking pots and griddles), and consumption (plates, bowls, and cups). Non-food-related ceramics include those used for decoration (vases, tiles, statuary, etc.), architectural purposes (bricks, roof tiles), and personal items (clay pipes, chamber pots, dolls, etc.). This division transcends the division between historic versus prehistoric ceramics and can often help determine the primary function of a site.

Although the archaeologist's question may apply equally to both prehistoric and historic ceramics, the concern for chronology often demands that they be analyzed separately. Fortunately, they are sufficiently distinctive that even the little-trained lab technician can tell the difference. By default, in the United States, prehistoric ceramics are presumed to have been made by Native American potters (pending verification of extraterrestrial visitation or early transoceanic trade). The historic ceramics found on archaeological sites are usually imported wares from England and the other colonial powers, although, especially after the eighteenth century, there was a rising number of local potteries of which the archaeologist must be aware. Regardless of their date and place of manufacture, the ceramic analyst must be familiar with a number of characteristics.

CERAMIC ATTRIBUTES

This discussion will focus on those attributes concerned with food-related ceramics. These artifacts comprise the bulk of the literature, though other types of ceramics will be discussed where appropriate. The primary characteristics considered here include composition, manufacturing technique and firing temperature, form, surface treatment, and decoration. The classification of these attributes into types will be discussed in a later section of this book.

The importance of various attributes to consider when analyzing ceramics differs somewhat between prehistoric and historic pottery. Different aspects of the paste or matrix of the vessel is considered important to the analysis of both types of pottery.

With prehistoric ceramics, the tempering material (material added to the clay to help bind it and prevent it from cracking during firing) is an important addition to the paste. The earliest ceramics were sometimes tempered with organic material such as in the fiber-tempered Late Archaic ceramics of Georgia or Florida. Other tempering agents include sand, grit, shell, and even bits of old ceramics (referred to as *grog-temper*). The St. John's series of aboriginal ceramics in North Florida appears temperless but actually is strengthened by nearly invisible sponge spicules that are part of the marine clay matrix. The importance of noting the type of temper used is that it is often a sensitive indicator of a pot's temporal and spatial placement in an archaeological sequence. A petrographic analysis of a ceramic's paste and temper (either under microscopic magnification or PIXE analysis) can even allow the archaeologist to trace the sherd to its clay source.

Historic ceramics, on the other hand, usually have no visible tempering agent. Here, it is the hardness and the color of the paste that are the defining characteristics. The color of the paste is indicative of the clay source and the firing temperature. The hardness or degree of vitrification (how glassy the paste becomes) is also dependent on the firing temperature. Degree of vitrification is a much more important characteristic for historic ceramics and is the basis for the further subdivision of this category (figure 8.3). Coarse earthenwares, refined earthenwares, stonewares, and porcelains were each fired at progressively hotter temperatures and thus increasingly vitreous (glassy) and impermeable to liquids.

The manufacturing techniques, especially in North America, differed greatly between Native American and European ceramics. Na-

WORKSHOP FOR HISTORIC CERAMICS

PROPERTIES
OF VARIOUS CERAMICS

EARTHENWARES	→	STONEWARES	→	PORCELAINS
opacity	→	increase in vitrification	→	transparency
1800 degrees F	→	increase firing temperature for maturity	→	2600 degrees F
impurities in clay	→	increase in alumina and water	→	purest clay
red/orange clay color	←	increase in iron and other impurities	←	white clay body
permeable	←	increase porosity	←	impermeable
upper strata clays	←	more accessible clays	←	deeper deposits

GLAZES
OF VARIOUS CERAMICS

EARTHENWARES	STONEWARES	PORCELAINS
lead-glaze (coarse & refined)	no glaze required	no glaze required
enamel or painted glaze (coarse & refined)	salt-glaze (coarse & refined)	enamel or painted
clay slips (coarse & refined)	clay slips (albany, bristol, etc. on coarse)	metal gilt
	alkaline glaze (coarse)	

chart compiled by
Linda F. Carnes-McNaughton
September 28, 1996

Figure 8.3 Physical properties of historic ceramics. (Prepared by Linda Carnes-McNaughton.)

tive ceramics, for the most part, were built using such techniques as coiling, molding, or modeling and were fired in open-air conditions (figure 8.4). European and Asian ceramics, on the other hand, were turned on potter's wheels and fired at higher temperatures in a kiln. The differing techniques of manufacture require that the ceramic analyst record different attributes for the two types of pottery.

Form is a basic category of any ceramic classification scheme. Prehistoric vessel forms can often be simply described as bowls, jars, bottles, or beakers. Historic ceramics can be described by these terms but also include plates, cups, and other terms that are more evocative of function such as serving platter or soup tureen. However, function is not always known for historic vessels, and at a basic level of classification a distinction is made between hollow wares (e.g., bowls) and flat wares (e.g., plates). Besides whole vessel form, usually the shape of different aspects of the vessel (e.g., lip, rim, neck, shoulder, body, and base) are described as well.

Surface treatment and decoration are two other important related, but separate, categories. Surface treatment is part of the manufacturing process of a pot. It includes such techniques as smoothing, burnishing, brushing, stamping, slipping (application of a thin liquid clay wash) and glazing. Historic ceramics were often glazed to make them

Figure 8.4   Open-air firing of ceramics. (Photo by C. Ewen.)

impermeable to liquids. In the United States, prehistoric ceramics were never glazed, although such surface treatments as slipping may have reduced their porosity.

Decoration applies to design elements added apart from the manufacturing process, though in some cases (such as with brushing or stamping) whether the treatment was functional or purely aesthetic is debatable. Prehistoric decoration elements were often stamped or incised on the clay before firing. Historic ceramics tended to rely on painted designs, transfer prints, or decals as their primary decoration.

The sort of measurements that should be taken of the ceramics in the assemblage can be as detailed as is necessary to answer the questions at hand. Generally, the size and volume of the vessel is approximated as closely as possible. This is done by determining the diameter of the vessel by matching the curve of a rim sherd on a chart of concentric circles (several styles of templates are commercially available). If enough of the vessel is present, then the height can be estimated. By calculating the volume of the cylinder ($\pi r^2 \times h$) a rough approximation of the vessel's volume can be achieved. Combining digital imagery with a powerful CADD package, not only can a more accurate volume estimate be made, but the computer can sometimes graphically reconstruct the entire vessel from a few sherds.

The preceding discussion merely scratches the surface of ceramic analysis. Literally dozens of books have been devoted to various aspects of ceramic analysis. However, a couple should be on the shelf of any archaeology lab. For prehistoric pottery, read Anna O. Shepard's (1980) classic *Ceramics for the Archaeologist*. First published in 1956 but reprinted and revised several times, this book discusses the basics: properties of the raw materials, techniques of manufacture, basic analytical techniques, classification, and interpretation. As comprehensive as Shepard's work is, it is certainly rivaled by Prudence Rice's (1987) encyclopedic *Pottery Analysis: A Sourcebook*. An individual with both works under his or her belt is well prepared to tackle any prehistoric pottery assemblage. Unfortunately, there are no similar treatises for their historic counterparts.

Works on historic ceramics tend to focus on a particular time period or nationality. Ivor Noël Hume (1978) makes a game try with his very useful *Guide to the Artifacts of Colonial America*, but the section of ceramics focuses primarily on English wares, and the time span is limited to the sixteenth through eighteenth centuries. George Quimby's (1980) edited volume, *Ceramics in America*, addresses many problems with ceramic analysis and interpretation, yet the larger subject matter with which the authors grapple, worldwide ceramic production, distribution, and use, is just too broad to be handled in a single volume. The analyst is encouraged to consult the literature on the time period and nationality of interest. For example, Kathleen Deagan's (1987) *Artifacts of the Spanish Colonies of Florida and the Caribbean, 1550–1800* is a good place to start for archaeologists working on Spanish sites in the southeastern United States and the Caribbean. Similar types of references exist for other regions and nationalities.

Ceramics can reveal much important information concerning an archaeological site. For example, the function of a site as well as the status of its inhabitants can be inferred from the ceramics recovered. Excavations at the sixteenth-century Spanish site of Puerto Real, Haiti, relied on ceramics to interpret the lives of their former owners. High proportions of hard-to-get imported wares delineated a neighborhood of wealthy individuals near the town plaza, whereas a prevalence of locally made wares of poorer quality on the outskirts of town defined the location of the town's lower economic class. Clandestine activity by one of the wealthy merchants was revealed by the presence of Chinese porcelain. This was only available from smugglers for most of the town's existence. Ceramics, both prehistoric and historic, can help determine a site's date of occupation, its place in the political geography of the region, whether it was engaged in long-distance trade, and even the descent system of the potters (see Longacre 1968). Some of the analytical techniques to derive these interpretations are discussed later in this volume.

METAL

Metal artifacts are most often associated with historic sites in North America. However, copper, lead (galena), silver, and gold appear on prehistoric sites as well, although their presence is relatively rare. The arrival of Europeans in the New World marks a sharp rise in the number and variety of metal artifacts on North American sites. The native inhabitants were ready customers for items made of metal, so that very early in the Colonial period metal items become fairly common on Native American sites. This sometimes makes it difficult to distinguish an historic Indian habitation from an early European homestead site on the basis of artifacts alone.

The most common metal to be introduced from Europe was iron, although artifacts made from copper and brass (an alloy of copper and tin), lead, pewter, silver, and gold were also available. Lead was molded into a variety of items, the most numerous of which were musket balls and other projectiles. The copper alloy, brass, was brought over as cooking vessels, hardware, and in sheet form, which the native peoples quickly adapted to their own uses. Copper, silver, and gold were part of the reason the Europeans came to the New World and were most often used in coinage and high-status artifacts. Various other metals and alloys such as aluminum, tin, and steel become more prevalent in later historic assemblages.

Iron has been fabricated into a bewildering array of artifacts ranging from swords to plowshares and everything in between. In fact, iron items represent so many different types of artifacts that it can be difficult to classify them. Ironically (pun intended), this popular metal is also highly corrosive and so the most common artifact to be recorded in this category is usually "unidentified iron flake or object."

Rather than basing this discussion of metal artifact analysis on the type of metal of which the artifact was made, it will probably be more useful to categorize them on the basis of the questions they can answer for the archaeologist. Among the many questions to which they might be applied, three common categories with potential for this type of artifact are as chronological indicators, as activity indicators, and as indicators of ethnicity and trade. Other possibilities include status indicators, questions relating to changes in technology, and acculturation studies.

Historic artifacts of all kinds lend themselves particularly well to questions of chronological placement, and metal artifacts are especially datable. Obviously, coins would seem a logical artifact for dating a site, yet the placing of a date on a coin is a relatively recent phenomenon. Fortunately, by using other clues (i.e., dating the reign of a monarch whose bust is featured on a coin), numismatists (e.g., Nesmith 1955) have been able to place most types of coins in a relatively narrow time frame.

Iron nails (Nelson 1963; Edwards and Wells 1994; Wells 2000) and barbed wire (Clifton 1970) have been used to roughly date sites. Nails can be chronologically divided on the basis of their method of manufacture (figure 8.5). Hand-wrought nails are the dominant type of nail until the early nineteenth century, when machine-cut nails (invented at the end of the eighteenth century) replace them in popularity. Cut nails are superceded at the end of the nineteenth century by modern wire nails. It should be noted, however, that because of recycling, distribution and other factors, these dates are truly rough approximations. However, since nails are often plentiful at many historic sites they can provide the excavator with a quick, general idea of the site's chronological placement.

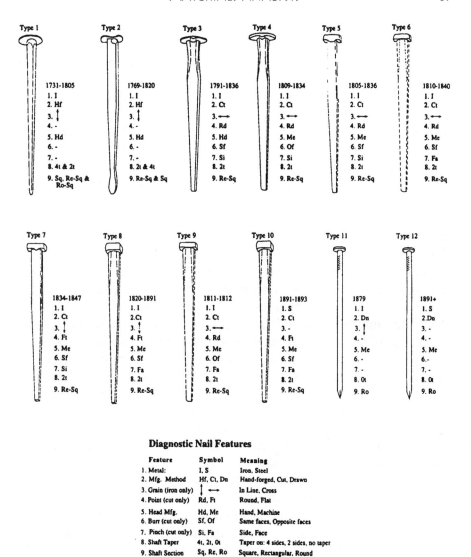

Figure 8.5 Nail chronology. (From Wells 1998. Reprinted by permission of the Society for Historical Archaeology.)

Another metal artifact that can be used to approximately date a site is the tin can, which is actually an iron container plated with tin to retard corrosion. Ubiquitous on historic sites (especially in the western United States) from the nineteenth century forward, metal containers are datable based on their method of sealing (Busch 1981; Rock 2000). These containers can reveal their contents and place of origin on the basis of their form and information that is often stamped on the can itself.

Weapons are yet another category of metal artifact whose development can be documented chronologically and which can often be traced to their place of manufacture. R. Ewart Oakeshott (1960) traces the development of weapons from the earliest atlatls and bows and arrows through use of metal in edged weapons to the development of firearms in his very readable *The Archaeology of Weapons: Arms and Armor from Prehistory to the Age of Chivalry*. Unfortunately for the North American historical archaeologist, he quits just before the discussion gets useful. It is difficult to find a single source (e.g., The Diagram Group 1980) that covers all weapons and ammunition of all nations, in the depth required by the archaeologist, from the sixteenth century to the present. Instead, the archaeologist must be more specific in the time and place of interest in order to find a suitable reference (e.g., Hamilton 1968, Brown 1980).

Questions of chronology are certainly not all that metal artifacts can answer. The function or primary activity taking place at a site is often revealed by the types of artifacts recovered. The recovery of farm implements could indicate agricultural activity; arms and ammunition might suggest a military site or evidence of hunting activity. Pins, needles, and thimbles could indicate domestic activity or even a commercial tailor's shop, depending on the quantity and context of such materials found (for an example, see South 1977:65–77).

Another important question that metal artifacts, like many other categories of historical artifacts, can answer is that of national origin and trade. With the proper references, many metal artifacts can be traced to their country and date of manufacture. Sometimes it is even possible to find the factory that made the item, the merchant that sold it, and the price he charged for it!

Where does one look to get information to identify metal artifacts or to learn about a particular class of artifact? Historical archaeologists are both blessed and cursed with a plethora of potential sources. For most labs, a selection of general secondary sources is usually the best way to start. Old catalogs, such as the Sears & Roebuck Catalog, are a good reference for many different items. It gives information concerning date (i.e., when the catalog was published), manufacturer, and price and usually has a picture of the item, thus making it a good identification tool. Collectors guides offer varying amounts of information on most kinds of artifacts and can be surprisingly specialized. If you can identify a specific type of artifact (e.g., farm implements), there is usually someone who collects it and probably at least one book on the topic (e.g., *Farm Tools through the Ages* 1973 by Michael Partridge).

These antique collectible books can be found at local and university libraries or even on-line at the Library of Congress (www.loc.gov) and are often available inexpensively through a variety of booksellers (e.g., www.amazon.com or www.barnes&noble.com). Finally, site reports and synthetic artifact guides (e.g., Hume 1978; South, Skowronek, and Johnson 1988) actually are written for the archaeologist and thus usually have the type of information in which the researcher is interested.

GLASS

Glass comprises another historic artifact category that became an instant hit with the native population of North America. Unlike most metals, glass is relatively stable and will survive with relatively little degradation (depending on its soda ash content) for long periods in most environments. Couple this with the fact that the manufacturer and contents of the bottle or jar were often molded onto the container, and one can see why historical archaeologists have devoted a great deal of study to glass artifacts.

The basic recipe for glass involves combining silica (sand), soda, and lime and heating until these ingredients fuse. This soda-lime glass is the most common type of glass, with variants depending on the proportions of the primary ingredients. Colors are the result of different impurities that were either intentionally or unintentionally added to the primary ingredients.

Although the constituent elements of glass have been known since the third millennium B.C., the techniques for working glass have evolved over time and became the jealously guarded secrets of various nations in the past. The results of this changing technology can inform the archaeologist of the origin and age of the glass artifacts that are recovered from a site (Lorrain 1968). Thus, for the analyst, it is important to observe whether the artifact has been free blown, mold blown, or machine made, as well as to note other descriptive characteristics.

Glass has been used to make a variety of artifacts including bottles, drinking vessels, window glass, and beads.

Glass beads are eagerly sought by archaeologists, especially those studying the early colonial period in North America since they were part of the trading truck brought by the first explorers (Smith and Good 1982; Karklins and Sprague 1980). Another useful form of glass artifact for the archaeologist are bottles. The evolution of the form these bottles took and their method of manufacture (blown vs. machine molded)

make them useful as chronological indicators on a site (see Fike 1987).
Containers of other sorts (e.g., drinking vessels and jars) are similarly
useful for dating sites, and flat glass can tell us more about a building
than just whether its windows were glazed.

One needn't be an expert in the history of glass to begin the basic
analysis of glass artifacts in an archaeological assemblage. A basic descriptive approach is recommended as a starting point for both novice
and experienced glass analysts.

Color is an important characteristic, which can deceive the unwary
observer. Dark glass, which may appear to be an opaque black at first
glance, often turns out to be a translucent olive-green or dark brown
when back-lit. For this reason, it is usually a good idea to discern
color by viewing the glass artifacts on a light table or against a light
colored background. The description of color can be standardized by
using a Munsell Book of Color or Pantone color wheel.

Another important descriptive attribute of glass is form. A basic division that can be made on small fragments, where the original artifact is not identifiable, is separating the fragments into flat versus
curved. This roughly distinguishes window from bottle glass; however, the generic terminology is necessary so that flat, case bottle glass
or curved drinking glass fragments are not misidentified. If larger,
identifiable pieces are present, the analyst may want to refer to a glass
nomenclature guide (e.g., Jones and Sullivan 1989 or White 1978) so
that the vessel and its constituent parts can be properly identified.

The function of the glass artifact can often be determined based on
its form and color. Once again, pertinent documentation is invaluable
in this regard (e.g., Brauner 2000; Jones and Sullivan 1989; Hume
1978). However, some types of glass artifacts have come in for more
study than others, due to their utility in dating sites or revealing the
nationality of their owner/maker.

Glass beads were one of the earliest trade items in North America.
Beads are made by three basic techniques: drawn cane, wire wound,
and mold blown. Drawn-cane beads, made by the simplest technique,
are formed by drawing a molten glass blob into a long tube or cane.
The cane is then cut into smaller lengths for individual beads. Often
these beads are further modified by tumbling with a polishing agent
over heat. The second common manufacturing technique is the winding method. Here, a thread of molten glass is wound around a rod
known as a *mandrel*. Once a suitable shape has been attained, the
bead is removed and allowed to cool or is further modified by being
pressed with a paddle (a technique known as *marvering*) or having ad-

ditional threads of different colored glass applied. Blown glass beads are comparatively rare. Their method of manufacture is characterized by the presence of a seam running down the side from the mold into which the glass was blown (figure 8.6).

The date and place of origin for many bead types are known and have been used as chronological marker artifacts to trace the routes of explorers, such as Hernando de Soto, through southeastern United States (e.g., Ewen 1998:85). A typology for North American trade beads has been developed (Kidd and Kidd 1983) and can serve as a useful classification system in the absence of more chronologically or culturally specific typologies (e.g., Deagan 1987:156–83; Smith and Good 1982; Karklins and Sprague 1980). A cautionary note: It should never be assumed that glass beads on native American sites represent direct contact with Europeans. Once acquired by the native population, these artifacts entered into another social interaction sphere and may have been traded over hundreds of miles to an individual who never saw a colonist.

Bottles and containers are another type of glass artifact archaeologists frequently study (e.g., Switzer 1974). They (especially bottles) can be dated on the basis of manufacturing technique, form (see Hume 1978:63–68,73), and method of closure. However, one should be careful to verify the dating methods being used as many early correlations,

Figure 8.6   Blown-glass beads. (Photo by Florida Bureau of Archaeological Research.)

such as the height of the kick-up or number of layers of patination (Demmy 1967), have not stood up under close scrutiny.

I will close this brief discussion of dating glass artifacts with a mention of window glass. Flat window glass is ubiquitous on historic sites after the eighteenth century. Historically, window panes were made in three different ways (Lorrain 1968). In the first method, the glass blower made a circular disc, called a *crown*, from which rectangular window panes were cut. This technique is discernable by a concentric pattern of small bubbles in the glass. An improved technique was to blow a cylinder of glass, which was then cut down the side and the reheated glass allowed to uncurl onto a flat surface. A casting method was also used for small panes or mirrors, but the need for subsequent polishing made this an expensive alternative. Attempts have been made to use the thickness of glass window panes to date sites (Roenke 1978). However, the applicability and utility of this method is somewhat limited, making it impractical in most cases.

The care and treatment of glass artifacts is a subject often ignored by archaeologists. The conventional wisdom is that as long as the artifact is carefully packed, it should curate indefinitely. However, if the glass has lain in a wet or alkaline environment, as with metal artifacts, it will start to decay. The decay, in this case, takes the form of exfoliation in iridescent layers. This devitrification cannot be reversed and any consolidation of the artifact should be left to a professional (Sease 1994:72–73). Final curation should be in a relatively dry environment in a padded case with rigid exterior walls.

As with the other sections on particular classes of artifact analysis, I have only scratched the surface here. Several references can assist glass artifact analysts with their questions. Two essential references are *The Parks Canada Glass Glossary for the Description of Containers, Tablewares, Flat Glass, and Closures* (Jones and Sullivan 1989) and the glass section in the SHA reader *Approaches to Material Culture Research for Historical Archaeologists* (Brauner 2000). Both references, and the references they contain, should get the lab personnel off on the right foot.

ORGANIC ARTIFACTS

Organic artifacts include such items as fabric, cordage, basketry, shell ornaments, bone tools, and wooden items. They are also commonly referred to as perishable artifacts and are usually found in very dry, very wet, or very cold conditions. Many of the artifacts that fall into this category will be those that will be flagged for immediate conservation or sent to a special analyst. Unmodified organic remains or ecofacts such as animal bone or floral specimens are usually the domain of zooarchaeology and paleoethnobotany, respectively. Human remains are dealt with by specially trained bioarchaeologists. Interpretations that can be gained from these items will be discussed in chapter 11.

Of paramount importance when dealing with perishable materials are their care and handling. If you do not take care of them up front, you may have nothing to analyze later! For the most part, these artifacts should not be cleaned by lab personnel any more than to brush off loose soil. Complete cleaning and consolidation are tasks best left to the special analyst. A task that the lab personnel can and should undertake is the complete recording of the fragile artifacts prior to analysis. This would include both drawing and photographing each artifact so that a complete record of its original appearance will exist should it be damaged by shipping or handling or even during conservation.

Storage of the artifact should be in the same environment in which it was found until it can be stabilized by a conservator. For example, wooden artifacts that have been recovered from a wet environment (e.g., dugout canoes recovered from a lakebed) should be kept immersed in water until proper permanent treatment can be undertaken. Smaller perishable artifacts, such as basketry from a bluffshelter site, should be sealed in a microenvironment (e.g., a plastic bag with a desiccant package) similar to the one in which they were found. At the very least, organic artifacts should be curated in a repository with temperature and humidity control.

Other than exercising extra care in handling, the analysis of perishable artifacts is similar to their more stable counterparts. For example, shell beads are described and measured in much the same way as glass or lapidary beads, with the addition of determining the species of shell being utilized. The same is true for all organic artifacts. Determining the species and element of the plant or animal from which the artifact is made is an important aspect of the description. This information will assist in the determination of the point of origin of the artifact and possibly the environment in which it was used.

Basketry and textiles warrant special consideration because their construction utilizes a different terminology which may be unfamiliar to the average archaeologist. A good source to have on hand when analyzing this class of artifact is *Basketry Technology: A Guide to Identification and Analysis* (Adovasio 1977). Adovasio (1977:1) relates basketry to textiles except that the former is more rigid and "manually assembled or woven without a frame or loom." He asserts that "basketry may be divided into three sub-classes of weaves that are mutually exclusive and taxonomically distinct: twining, coiling and plaiting." He goes on to discuss examples of these methods and illustrates them as well. Another good, brief discussion of the analysis of textiles and basketry is found in *Archaeology Laboratory Methods* (Sutton and Arkush 1998: chapter 8). The archaeologist is also urged to consult the literature in the area in which they are working for comparative information. This is especially important when attempting to classify artifacts and fit them into an existing regional chronological sequence.

9

CLASSIFICATION

The rough sorting procedure of separating artifacts into the material categories discussed in the previous chapter represents a simple exercise in classification. An archaeological classification system or typology is simply an ordering of artifacts into classes or types according to a prescribed system on the basis of their attributes. An *attribute* is a well-defined feature of an artifact, such as color, that cannot be further subdivided. There are several kinds of attributes an archaeologist looks for in an artifact, which can be grouped into three macrocategories: stylistic, formal, and technological. An example of a technological attribute would be the kind of chert from which a projectile point was made. The design motif on a ceramic vessel is an example of a stylistic attribute, whereas the shape of the vessel itself (i.e., bowl, jar, etc.) would be a formal attribute.

In 1736, Carolus Linnaeus published *Systema Naturae*, which presented a classification system or taxonomy for all living things. While there has been some tinkering with its structure, it has generally withstood the test of time and most biologists, if not entirely happy with it, have at least come to accept its utility. As mentioned earlier, there is no archaeological equivalent to the Linnaean taxonomy, and given the diversity of opinions and interests among modern scholars, it is easy to understand why. One wonders how successful Linnaeus would be if he were to propose his scheme today!

One of the biggest obstacles to devising a classification scheme is its scope. The challenge is to make it comprehensive enough to include all the different data categories that might be of interest to the archaeologist, without having the system become so cumbersome that it actually impedes the interpretation of the artifact assemblage. Another important consideration is that the classification system have enough rigidity in its structure to ensure compatibility across datasets, while retaining the flexibility to allow the individual archaeologist to use it to answer questions peculiar to a single site or research design. This is a tall order and one that many institutions are rethinking as they move to computerize their databases.

OBJECTIVES

In designing a classification scheme, it is important always to remember the basic goals that the system is designed to achieve. This advice might seem obvious, but it is easy to lose track of the purpose of the endeavor when in the throes of subdividing artifact categories and wrestling with producing the user's manual for your laboratory's database program. So, it is important to think of the big picture of classification before, during, and after the design of your system.

The purpose of a classification system is to organize the data into manageable units—that is, to bring some semblance of order to the pile of artifacts spread out on your lab table. Once there is a logical order to the assemblage, you can begin to see patterns or correlations among different categories of your data. Which attributes occur together and which do not? The data categories include not only the composition of the artifact but also its form, function, decoration, age, and provenience, to name but a few of the fields the archaeologist must consider.

The process of classification began with the rough sorting into material categories that was done during the artifact processing stage. The next step is to subdivide these rough categories into meaningful archaeological classes. This will be the basis for relating or separating specific groups of artifacts. Once these categories are defined, then the analyst can attempt to discern relationships between the categories. Take, for example, a hypothetical artifact assemblage from a multicomponent site. Within this assemblage, you create a category for ceramics. This category can further be divided into prehistoric and historic. These categories can be even further divided, by surface treatment, into glazed and unglazed. Looking at relationships among categories reveals that only the historic ceramics are glazed. This is a simple example that nevertheless demonstrates the importance of a well-constructed database for the analysis of an artifact assemblage.

For an example of a more elaborate ceramic typology, see figure 8.3 in the previous chapter's discussion of ceramic analysis.

As stated at the beginning of this book, artifact analysis involves both the organization and description of your data. Description is the key to a good archaeological site report. A report in which an artifact assemblage has been completely misinterpreted or a key artifact misidentified can still be a valuable tool if the data have been well described. The important attributes to be described vary among the artifact classes. Some of these attributes were discussed in the previous section; others will be discussed later. In any event, it is important to be as objective as possible in your description of the artifact assemblage. The organization of your data tends to be somewhat more subjective.

EMIC VERSUS ETIC

A fundamental dispute in the construction of archaeological classification schemes revolves around the perspective taken by the archaeologist. Do the classificatory categories reflect the interests of the archaeologist (the outsider's or etic perspective), or do they reflect the categories that the people who made the artifacts had in mind (the emic or insider's perspective)? In other words, should we take the etic perspective and arrange the artifacts in an order that fits the past into a framework that is familiar to us, or should we attempt to take the emic perspective and view the artifacts as would the culture that made them? This was the essence of the Ford–Spaulding debate in the 1950s, an exchange that presaged the postprocessual paradigm by more than thirty years.

Albert Spaulding (1953) claimed that the classification of types should be a process of discovery of the combinations of attributes favored by the makers, not an arbitrary procedure of the classifier. Thus, in the true emic mode, classification should be independent for each cultural context. That is, each project should have its own classification scheme. To arrive at the emic perspective, statistical techniques would be used to discover combinations of two or more attributes meaningful to the maker. This is the essence of some types of multivariate analyses performed by archaeologists today.

James Ford (1954) responded that since culture itself is an etic construct, we would be deluding ourselves to think that reaching an emic perspective is even possible. He claimed that Spaulding's statistical analyses would reveal only the degree to which people followed a particular style at a particular point in time. The type thus "discovered" would not be useful for reconstructing a diachronic culture history. He further claimed that there were two reasons why Spaulding's techniques would not discover true emic types. First, at that time (and one could argue the same is true of today's archaeology) there simply wasn't sufficient chronological control to use the data the way in which Spaulding intended. Second, even if artifacts could be precisely placed in time, the nature of culture change is that it is not always gradual and can be affected by a variety of factors that defy prediction.

Undaunted, Spaulding (1954) replied by asking what Ford meant by "historically useful," indicating that he felt that Ford had missed the point of what he was trying to accomplish, which was not reconstructing culture history in the way that Ford understood it. He also added that any reasonably consistent and well-defined behavior pattern was historically useful. Spaulding clarified his concept of archaeological typology by claiming that there were actually three levels of types, each successive level building on the previous level and eventually revealing functional types. He countered Ford's claim that his belief that cluster analysis would automatically produce emic types was naive. He responded that his statistical tests merely revealed significant clusters of attributes. It was up to the archaeologist to interpret what these combinations meant.

Ultimately, and this is as true today as when the debate raged through the pages of the *American Anthropologist*, the debate is not really about categories but about questions. Comparing Spaulding's types with Ford's is like comparing apples to oranges—they were designed to answer different questions. Ford was interested in building a spatial-temporal framework for the lower Mississippi Valley, whereas Spaulding was interested in understanding how particular past peoples thought at a particular point in time. One could argue that Ford was promoting paleoethnology (the comparative study of past cultures), while Spaulding championed paleoethnography (the study of a particular past culture). Willey and Phillips (1958:13) in their classic *Method and Theory in American Archaeology* attempted to resolve the debate by claiming that Ford and Spaulding were both right. All archaeologically defined types were likely to possess some degree of correspondence to what a society would classify as the "right way" to make an artifact. They felt that the goal of a typology was to make the correspondence between "created" and "discovered" types as close as possible.

The challenge for the contemporary archaeologist faced with an artifact assemblage or multiple assemblages is to devise a classificatory structure that can be used to investigate both emic and etic questions. The availability of high-speed, high-capacity personal computers makes the use of complex hierarchical databases easy and practical. Statistical tests that would have taken Spaulding weeks merely to gather the pertinent data, let alone perform the calculations, can now be undertaken in a matter of minutes from existing databases.

The following section is not meant to show the reader the "right way" to classify artifacts. Rather, it is a demonstration of how other archaeologists have approached the problem of archaeological classification and the variables to be considered in this undertaking.

CLASSIFICATION SCHEMES

Depending on the questions to be asked of the data, artifacts can be classified in a number of different ways. Most classification systems are constructed on the basis of multiple attributes arranged hierarchically. There are many different basic categories to be considered for the classification of artifacts from any archaeological project.

MATERIAL/TECHNOLOGICAL

As discussed previously, the material from which an artifact is made is often the most basic means of subdividing the archaeological assemblage. It allows for a preliminary sorting of the artifacts by inexperienced personnel and provides the archaeologist with a quick assessment of the range of artifacts present. It gives a thumbnail sketch of whether the site consists mostly of lithic artifacts or whether pottery or historic materials are present. It is also useful for separating out artifacts that require stabilization (e.g., iron and perishable artifacts) as well as those artifacts that might undergo specialized analyses at another laboratory (e.g., faunal and floral remains, human skeletal remains, radiocarbon samples, etc.). Other categories will require more informed observation by a trained lab technician.

FORMAL/MORPHOLOGICAL

Another basis for separating and combining groups of artifacts is by their form or shape. In a hierarchically based system, artifacts within certain categories (such as materials) are often subdivided on the basis of their shapes. For example, in the discussion of glass artifacts in chapter 8, we saw that they could be divided into flat and curved fragments. This is a basically descriptive approach that is most often employed when the function of the artifact is not known. These descriptions are based primarily on the measurable attributes of the artifact such as height, width, length, thickness, and weight.

A good example of a subdivision based on form would be in the ceramic category. Here the form category could be subdivided on the basis of whole vessels and fragments or sherds. Sherds are usually described by their form and perceived location on the whole vessel. Most archaeologists employ such descriptive categories as rim, base, shoulder, and appendage when describing the ceramic subassemblage. These elements can be further detailed by such terms as *everted rim, conoidal base, incised shoulder*, or *effigy handle*, to name a few.

Whole vessels are rarely found outside of a burial context on most archaeological sites since if they weren't broken, they wouldn't have been thrown away! However, it is often possible to extrapolate the form of the vessel from a large sherd or series of sherds that have been reconstructed in the lab. Forms of whole vessels would include such basic descriptive categories as bowls, beakers, jars, plates, and cups or dippers. Historic vessel form descriptions may be even more elaborate, including platter, tumbler, tea cup, goblet, and tureen, to name a few. One should note, especially with historic form descriptions, that often a function is implied. This can provide the basis for another artifact categorization discussed below.

FUNCTIONAL

Functional artifact categories can be either useful or misleading. They are potentially the most power-interpretive categories that an archaeologist can devise for reconstructing past lifeways at a particular site. The function of the majority of the artifacts at a site often reveals the site's overall function as well (e.g., hunting camp, lithic extraction, domestic structure, ceremonial center, etc.). Defining the function of an object is supposed to be one of the skills that an archaeologist has over the layman.

The functions of various artifacts are derived, in the case of prehistoric artifacts, from using ethnographic analogy, replication experiments, or the direct historic approach using ethnohistoric accounts of early explorers. For example, the bannerstone or atlatl weight has no real correlate in modern Western society. However, reference to prehistoric pictographs and early accounts of tribal peoples suggests these artifacts were associated with spear-throwing devices. Replication experiments corroborate this interpretation.

Even with the corpus of ethnographic data at hand, interpretation is not always possible. Artifacts whose function had eluded the archaeologist despite their use of these investigative techniques were in the past sometimes referred to as "ceremonial objects" or items of "religious significance" to hide the classifier's ignorance. One of the unforeseen consequences of these unsupported speculations is that sacred artifacts are eligible for immediate repatriation to descendant Native American groups under the Native American Graves Protection and Repatriation Act (NAGPRA). Today most archaeologists simply describe such objects and list their functions as "unknown" rather than speculating. Other impacts of federal legislation will be discussed elsewhere in this volume.

These examples illustrate the rewards and perils of the functional categorization of artifacts. Often the function of an artifact is not known or assumed functions are either wrong or highly conjectural. For example, ceramic disks found on both historic and prehistoric sites are usually referred to as *gaming pieces*. There is usually no explanation of what the game might have been or how these disks might have functioned as part of the game other than as wagering tokens. This might be seen as harmless speculation on the part of archaeologists who just can't stand to have unidentified artifacts in their catalogs. However, these baseless speculations often get repeated again and again in the literature until they are eventually reified as "the truth" and potentially mislead all subsequent investigations.

There is yet another pitfall in the use of functional groups for artifact classification. Many, if not most, artifacts had multiple functions. Who among us has not used a pocketknife to tighten a screw or mason's trowel to excavate a feature? The multipurpose nature of various tools must have been even greater during the prehistoric period. However, there are ways, such as use wear analysis (see the "Lithics" section in chapter 8) to determine the *primary* use of many tools. Thus, some archaeologists have made productive use of this category of classification. This has been especially true in historical archaeology where many artifacts have a modern equivalent and so their function is better understood by the archaeologist.

One of the pioneers and principal exponents of functional artifact categories in historical archaeology was Stanley South. His explicit purpose for formulating these functional groups was so that he could identify "activities related to the systemic context reflected by the archaeological record" (South 1977:93). These functional categories were then used to detect patterns of regularity and variability in the site's assemblage that might be used inductively to generate statements of theory.

A modified version of South's artifact categories (table 9.1) was used to classify the artifacts recovered from the sixteenth-century Spanish site of Puerto Real, Haiti (Ewen 1991:61). The purpose of these groups was to provide a meaningful organization of the artifact assemblage in terms of human behavior as well as a basis for inter- and intrasite comparison. In this case, comparisons were made with previously excavated portions of Puerto Real as well as with sites in St. Augustine, Florida. The ceramic assemblage was subdivided into table wares and utilitarian wares so as to assess change through time as well as to use it as an index for measuring status differences within the community. The result was the successful test of a material model for Spanish Colonial adaptation to the New World (Ewen 1991:115–18).

South was cognizant of the aforementioned pitfalls of a functional classification scheme:

> Since virtually any class of artifacts can be seen to possibly serve a variety of purposes within the past cultural context, it is foolhardy to attempt to

Table 9.1. Artifact Categories at Puerto Real	
Group	Artifact Category
1	Majolica
2	European Utilitarian Ceramics
3	Non-Majolica European Tablewares
4	Locally Made Ceramics
5	Kitchen
6	Structural Hardware
7	Arms and Armor
8	Clothing Related
9	Personal Items
10	Activity
11	Unidentified Metal Objects
12	Masonry
13	Furniture Hardware
14	Tools
15	Toys and Games
16	Harness and Tack
17	Religious
18	Miscellaneous
19	Unaffiliated
20	Hispanic Tablewares

arrive at a classification that has no exceptions. For this reason the artifact classifications used here are considered adequate for a wide range of historic sites. There is nothing wrong, of course, in expanding the list . . . in the face of a research design demanding such an addition. (South 1977:96)

Prehistoric archaeologists have not embraced such a classification system as enthusiastically, perhaps because, as previously noted, prehistoric artifacts are not as well understood as their historic counterparts. A notable exception is Howard Winters's (1968:184) use of functional categories for categorizing grave goods in an attempt to define a pattern that would reflect a value system for the Indian Knoll Culture (a Late Archaic manifestation in Kentucky). These artifact categories were grouped into three general classes: (1) items classifiable as general utility tools, weapons, fabricating and processing tools, and domestic implements and ornaments manufactured from locally available raw materials; (2) items generally classified as ceremonial equipment; (3) ornamental items occurring in special, segregated contexts, that are manufactured from rare materials and may serve utilitarian or ceremonial functions. Winters's categories represented values that could be inferred from their function and the raw material from which they were made. Combining simple statistical analysis with ethnohistoric data, Winters made a compelling case for the utility of this classificatory scheme for prehistoric data.

STYLISTIC

A popular approach to the classification of artifacts is on the basis of their stylistic qualities. Stylistic attributes include color, decoration, and surface finish (e.g., Munsell value 10YR 3/4, cord-marked, burnished, respectively). Prehistoric and historic pottery types are often distinguished chronologically by their stylistic attributes. Mississippian pottery is characterized by the stylistic motifs on the vessels as are the transfer-printed ceramics from the Staffordshire potteries.

The previously discussed Ford–Spaulding debate was primarily concerned with the interpretive utility of stylistic attributes. Different design elements characterize different time periods or cultural groups. In north Florida, the late prehistoric Fort Walton complex of ceramics are distinguished by incised, curvilinear designs, whereas the later Lamar-influenced Leon Jefferson series have stamped designs on the surface of the pottery. This stylistic change, interpreted as extraregional in origin, has been used as a chronological marker by archaeologists in the area.

CHRONOLOGICAL

A specialized typology can be built around these temporally sensitive or "diagnostic" artifacts. This classification would include types
defined by form that are time markers. Such artifacts as Clovis points
or machine-cut nails are used by archaeologists in the same manner
that a paleontologist would use index fossils.

A good example of how artifacts have been used as diagnostic time
markers is at the site of Puerto Real, Haiti. The site, occupied by the
Spanish colonists from 1504 to 1578, was divided into two periods of
occupation: early and late. It was possible to distinguish the Early Period (pre-1550) from the Late Period (post-1550) occupation primarily
on the basis of the presence of such material marker artifacts as
Cologne stoneware and Ming porcelain. Historical records indicate
that these wares were not available in the Caribbean prior to 1550.
Thus, combining these index artifacts with stratigraphic analyses permitted the deposits to be placed in one of two chronological contexts.

FOLK TAXONOMIES

Folk taxonomies are what Spaulding was after, classification systems derived by the people that made the artifacts. Ethnologists
record these as a basic part of their data collecting when in the field.
Unfortunately, without a time machine, archaeologists can't directly
gather these data. However, archaeologists have derived methods for
indirectly arriving at these categories.

The previously discussed artifact classification systems employ a
primarily etic perspective. That is, the categories are determined by
the archaeologist with little regard for the thoughts of the people who
made the artifact. Yet, trying to gain an insider's perspective on the
past is arguably one of the basic goals of archaeology. Albert Spaulding used statistical techniques in an attempt to elicit the attributes
of pottery made the "right" way in the past. Historical archaeology,
with the added dimension of historical records, can make a more direct inference from artifact categories.

Archaeologists in the Chesapeake region of Maryland and Virginia
have developed a folk taxonomy for ceramics (Beaudry et al. 1983).
The Potomac Typological System (with the clever acronym of POTS)
links vessel forms with terms used in probate inventories and other
colonial documents. Specifically, the authors intended to "begin to
systematize the terms in the categories used to describe excavated ce-

ramic vessels and the assemblages they comprise, in a way that will make the cultural dynamics behind them more accessible" (Beaudry et al. 1983:17)—in other words, to conduct middle-range research connecting the archaeological record with past behavior.

The Sears & Roebuck catalog is a commercial classification system with items divided by function, style, and technological criteria. Using past records like the Sears catalog of one hundred years ago, archaeologist can arrange their artifacts on the basis of cost and popularity.

These folk taxonomies are not better than the previously discussed typologies. They merely represent another perspective on the past that can help to answer a different suite of questions.

QUANTIFICATION

It has been said that if you can't quantify it, it doesn't exist. To the archaeologist, who must deal with the material remains of the past, this is especially true. So the question becomes not whether you can quantify it but how.

COUNTS

The most obvious way to quantify your artifacts is to count them. Usually the artifacts will be summarized by whichever categories they have been divided into and then those categories combined to produce a grand total of artifacts recovered from the site. For various analytical procedures, however, simple counts are not sufficient.

Ceramics is a good example of a category for which simple sherd counts are not always the best means of quantification. In some cases, sherd counts can actually be misleading! For example, two pots of identical size but having different decoration are broken. One breaks into twenty-five pieces, while the other yields fifty sherds. On the basis of this simple count of the sherds, the analyst would conclude that there were twice as many pots of the second type as of the first. This discrepancy might be obvious on the basis of sherd size when dealing with just two vessels, but when the archaeologist is confronted with hundreds or thousands of sherds, these discrepancies become less apparent. Other factors that affect sherd count include vessel size and durability of the ceramic vessel. A small stoneware bowl will break into fewer pieces than a large porcelain vase.

The archaeologist can deal with the potentially skewing affects of raw artifact counts in a couple of ways. One simple approach to correct the bias inherent in fragment size is to weigh the fragments. Thus, pots of similar size and composition would have similar weights no matter how fragmented they became. Digital scales make relatively painless the acquisition of these data, which can, with the proper equipment, be entered directly into a computerized database.

A more labor-intensive but potential valuable alternative means of quantification that addresses the issue of vessel size and durability is the estimation of the minimum number of vessels. In zooarchaeology, this statistic is referred to as the *minimum number of individuals* (MNI) and is a standard way of quantifying faunal remains. Realizing that most of a skeleton does not survive the taphonomic processes that intervene between deposition and intervention, zooarchaeologists have derived a method of determining the minimum number of animals present in the assemblage that would account for all the bones in the assemblage. This is based on the most numerous unique element (e.g., right tibia) of each species.

The ceramic equivalent of the MNI would be a minimum vessel count. This entails the examination of all sherds and separating them on the bases of distinctive morphological and stylistic attributes. This obviously involves a lot of refitting work in the lab, with the focus on the distinctive elements of the ceramics such as the rim, base, and decorative elements. A number of potential complications (e.g., how does one deal with matched sets of historic ceramics?) may arise with this method of quantification. Yet for some analytical techniques, estimated vessel counts are essential.

While discussing quantification, it is appropriate to consider the scale to be used for measurement. For most archaeologists, this is a question of the metric versus the English system. Although the United States (and Burma) steadfastly resist the metric system, most prehistoric archaeologists have adopted this system for their projects and so take their measurements in grams, liters, and centimeters. Historical archaeologists, on the other hand, often opt for the English system of feet and inches (or an engineer's scale of feet and tenths of a foot). This is because most English colonial and postcolonial sites in North America were constructed using the English system. The system of measurement should be made with an eye toward compatibility with other data sets and the availability of the proper equipment.

DATABASES

Once the classification system has been established and the method of quantification decided, it is necessary to create a means of quickly retrieving these data. It does little good to fill out reams of catalog sheets that have recorded the many variables of each artifact that you deem important if you have to laboriously scrutinize and retally each entry every time you have a question of the assemblage.

For example, say that you have recovered thirty thousand artifacts from a Late Woodland period village site in North Carolina. You are able to lump some of the artifacts into broader categories in your typology so you might have eighteen thousand entries on your artifact inventory sheets. Each sheet has twenty-five entries. If you wanted to tabulate all of the shell-tempered pottery from your assemblage, you would have to manually sort through all 720 sheets of the inventory to answer this simple question. If you wanted to know how many of these were rims, you'd have to repeat your search on the sheets that had contained shell-tempered ceramics.

Obviously this is a very labor-intensive and error-prone process (i.e., after a couple of hundred sheets, you might overlook an entry). The larger the artifact assemblage, the more time each search will take and the more likely errors will be made. Archaeologists have long sought a more efficient way to organize and retrieve their data.

CARD CATALOGS

Library card catalogs offered a workable system that was emulated by many archaeologists. The pertinent attribute data for an artifact, or groups of similar artifacts, could be placed on index cards along with provenience data. In other words, each entry from the catalog sheet was put on a separate card that could then be sorted by the archaeological analyst, such as by an attribute (e.g., composition) or provenience (e.g., unit 10, level 2).

A limitation of this system was that you could only sort on one attribute at a time, though it was fairly easy to create subsets. Returning to our Woodland village example, once you had pulled all the cards with shell-tempered pottery, you could quickly thumb through those cards to find the rim sherds (assuming you had recorded that information!). Still, searching on multiple variables was time-consuming.

A variation on the card cataloging scheme used at the University of Florida in the late 1970s involved using cards that had holes along their edges with a number printed beneath each hole. The numbers corresponded to artifact attributes (e.g., 10 = ceramic, 25 = shell tempered, 36 = rim). The holes with the numbers corresponding to the attributes possessed by the artifacts were punched open on the card. To find the artifact with attributes desired would involve running a spindle through the hole of the attribute desired. Upon raising the spindle, the cards having the artifacts with the desired attributes would drop out. This low-tech approach, while far from perfect, did speed analysis time considerably.

ELECTRONIC DATA

Computers are the most efficient way to process text, graphics, and data related to your site. Yes, they crash, develop odd glitches, and some programs are difficult to learn, but all these problems can be said to pertain to automobiles as well, and no one is still using horses for basic transportation! Every week computer technology gets faster, more powerful, easier to use, and less expensive. Today, powerful desktop units that rival the computing power of the mainframe computers of twenty years ago are well within the reach of even the most modest archaeological lab. The power of the computer is especially evident in its ability to take large quantities of disparate data and quickly sort them in a variety of ways.

It is difficult to write about specific computer solutions when that particular computer platform or software program is likely to be obsolete by the time this manuscript is published. Still, it is possible to give some general guidelines for computer applications that will apply no matter what system is in place.

Today it is possible to store large databases on a relatively inexpensive desktop computer. Many institutions are putting their entire lab's inventory on a single machine with removable storage capabilities. Powerful relational database programs allow the archaeologist to access more than one data set at a time. One file can hold the provenience data, while another contains the artifact inventory, and still another might hold images of the artifacts themselves. These data sets are linked through a common variable such as the FS number. What's more, the desired data can be quickly retrieved and manipulated with various statistical programs. Choosing the proper hardware and software for this task is an endeavor that should not be lightly undertaken.

The necessary computer hardware is the most difficult to predict. Choose a platform (e.g., Windows, Mac, Unix, etc.) that will run the currently desired programs. It is extremely difficult to predict the future of any computer company, so buy the machine that will accomplish what you want done today, not what you think you might want in the future. One caveat: Always buy the newest technology you can afford. Buying yesterday's technology may be cheaper, but it will often not run the programs you want today, let alone any future upgrades.

Storage media are difficult to predict as well. When I was at the Arkansas Archeological Survey, I ran across several boxes of keypunched computer cards. I was told they were from several past projects that were being stored in case someone wanted to reanalyze the data. Of course, that archaeologist would have had to go to the Smithsonian to find a card reader to upload the data into a computer! We ended up recycling the paper cards.

Everyone knows stories of data that are no longer retrievable because the storage media is obsolete. My master's thesis is on an eight-inch floppy disk. A colleague has his dissertation on an old Osborne computer running CPM. Computers that can read 5¼-inch floppy disks will be completely extinct by the time this book is published. The only solution is to continually transfer your data to the new industry standard as it becomes available and to *always print a hard copy of your data.* In a worst-case scenario, you can always reenter the data.

Database software is just as prone to obsolescence. The major question the lab director must confront is whether to go with a dedicated or commercial program. That is, should the database program be tailored to your particular lab, or should you buy a program that other archaeologists elsewhere are using? The answer to this question depends on how much outside support is required by the user. An organization with a great deal of in-house tech support can develop and maintain database software that fits their needs and computer hardware. The UNIX-based DELOS database used by the Arkansas Archeological Survey is a good example of a dedicated database (figure 9.1).

Organizations without extensive computer staff might want to consider purchasing a commercially available database (e.g., Access or Filemaker) or spreadsheet program (e.g., Excel or Quattro Pro) and simply develop their own data structure and program scripts for generating reports. This method presupposes a certain degree of computer literacy to design and implement the database structure, and limited tech support is possible from the commercial vendor of that program. Many large university labs and state programs have opted for this approach.

DELOS Artifact Inventory Form

Site Number _3PU256_   Site Name _Ashley_   Recorder _J. Pebworth_   Date Encoded _____

Accession Number _84-518_   Project Number _00-03_   Analyst _J. Pebworth_   Date Entered _2/10/00_ mw

PRH	LSN	ASN	PM	General	Specific	Material	Weight	Count					Morpho Funct	Qualifier	Location	Type/Variety	1	2	3
128	1	1	H	EUCER	RMBAS	PORC	56g	2					Bowl	EMBSD LAV					
128	1	2	H	EUCER	HNDL	IWARE	10.4g	1					BOWL	B2N TRN					
128	1	3	H	EUCER	RMBDY	REWARE	13.3g	1											
128	1	4	H	EUCER	RMBAS	PORC	39.1g	2					Bowl	DWK GILT					
128	1	5	H	EUCER	RMBAS	REWARE	21.2g	1					Bowl	DECAL					
128	1	6	H	EUCER	HNDL	PORC	13.7g	1											
128	1	7	H	EUCER	RIM	RWARE	2.8g	1					PLATTR	GRN SCALP SACLL					
128	1	8	H	EUCER	RMBDY	RWARE	14.3g	1					PLATE	BLU SHELL					
128	1	9	H	EUCER	RMBDY	IWARE	26.9g	1					Bowl	BARRED PNK GILT	✓				
128	1	10	H	EUCER	Body	RWARE	33.6g	1					BOTTLE	SENSIP SAL	BASE	INK ROSENERSON			
128	1	11	H	EUCER	RMBDY	YWARE	145g	2					MBOWL	AIK CIR AL BR	✓				
128	1	12	H	EUCER	BOBASE	SWARE	144.1g	3						AL					
128	1	13	H	EUCER	RMBDY	EWARE	193.6g	4					MBowl	CIR AL					
128	1	14	H	EUCER	Body	EWARE	65.6g	1						PNK AL					
128	1	15	H	EUCER	Body	SWARE	6.2g	1						DR AL					
128	1	16	H	EUCER	Body	EWARE	7.2g	1						CIR AL					
128	1	17	H	EUCER	Base	IWARE		1						BURNED					

Figure 9.1   DELOS data sheet. (Courtesy of the Arkansas Archeological Survey.)

Another option is a generic archaeological database program that can be used as is or customized to suit a particular lab's needs. These programs (e.g., Minark, WinRelic, Re:discovery) are specifically geared to archaeologists, and the level of support is variable. Training in the use of these programs is sometimes available. The most compelling reason to go this particular route is that a professional programmer has developed this program specifically for archaeologists and has written a user interface that allows even technophobic archaeologists or untrained undergraduates to enter and retrieve data.

An example of this last approach to computerized databases is the Re:discovery database, which my lab recently acquired. I will use this merely as an example of how one lab went about computerizing their artifact collections. Working with the Re:discovery programmers, we developed a provenience database based on the excavation level sheets used by our students in the field (figure 9.2). This was linked to our artifact inventory database by the FS number field (figure 9.3). We have also linked our lab's site accession log by transferring it to a site record database (figure 9.4). Future additions being contemplated include an image database and map catalog.

A new type of database management, which will no doubt come to dominate the field, are on-line databases. The National Archaeological Database (www.cast.usark.edu/products/NADB/) is an on-line database of databases including a bibliography of CRM reports, information concerning NAGPRA, and regional GIS maps. In England, the

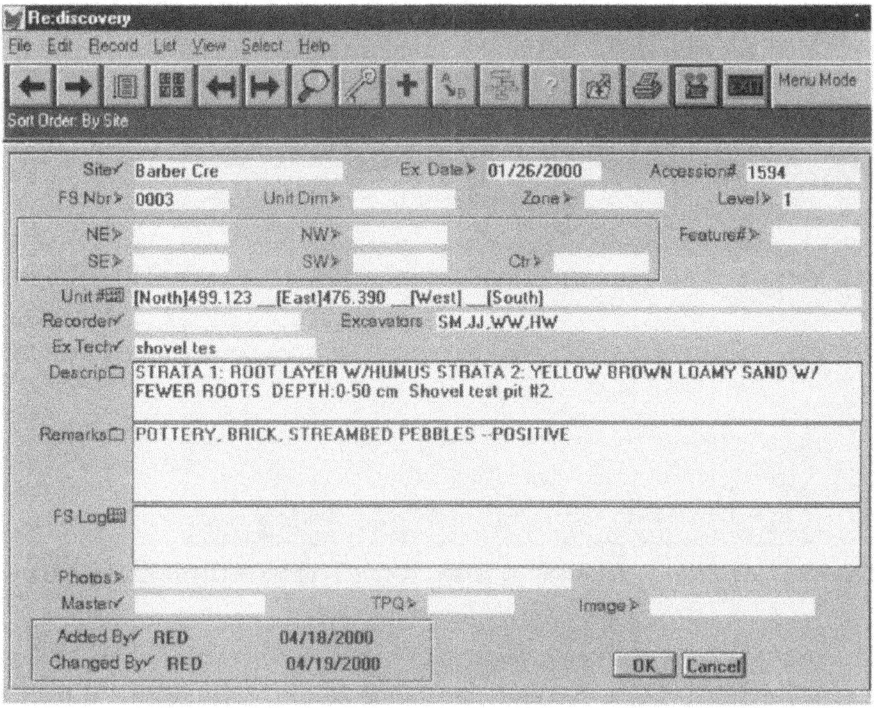

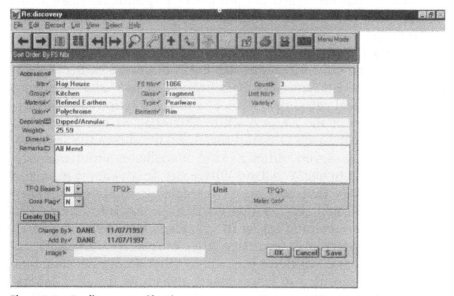

Figure 9.2 Re:discovery context screen. (Courtesy of the ECU Archaeology Lab.)

Figure 9.3 Re:discovery artifact inventory screen. (Courtesy of the ECU Archaeology Lab.)

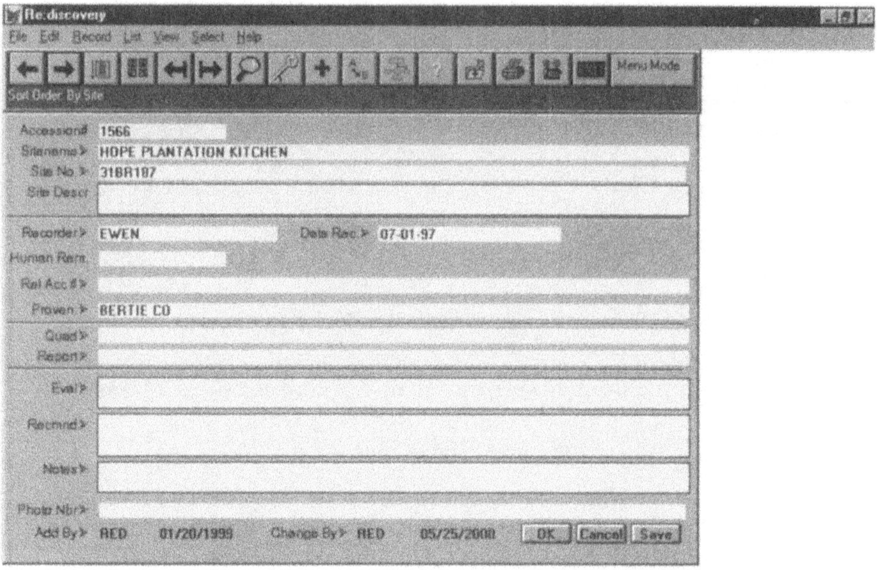

Figure 9.4   Re:discovery accession log screen. (Courtesy of the ECU Archaeology Lab.)

Archaeological Data Service (ads.ahds.ac.uk/project/general.html)
will archive archaeological databases and make them available on-
line for a modest fee. While not promoting a specific database architecture, they do advocate standard vocabulary for the artifact
inventory.

The artifact inventory is the heart of the database and uses many of
the different types of categories (table 9.2) discussed earlier. For instance, "Group" is a functional classification. "Class" and "Element"
are morphological categories. "Color" and "Decoration" refer to stylistic attributes of the artifact, while "Material" is a technological
category. The database's powerful search engine allows the archaeologist to search on several different kind of attributes simultaneously.
Returning again to our Woodland Village site, it is a simple matter to
construct a query that asks for all the ceramic rims that are shell
tempered. You could also ask that it limit the search to feature contexts. Your answer would appear in seconds. It would also supply all
the related contextual information (e.g., excavation unit, level, related contexts) and attributes (e.g., color, other decorative elements,
etc.) that you specified in your request and prints it out in tabular
form or imports it to your word processor for insertion into the final
report.

Table 9.2. Database Structure for East Carolina University Archaeology Laboratory	
Group:	Functional categories following South (1977). Other categories can be added (i.e., for prehistoric assemblages or special research questions) as needed by the archaeologist.
Class:	This category is loosely based on artifact form and follows South's categories when the artifact is whole. Otherwise, it is more prudent to enter "fragment" if the artifact is not complete, especially when referring to ceramics and glass. Nails, spikes, and staples would be referred to as "fastener" in this field.
Material:	Refers to the composition of the artifact.
Type:	Similar to South's category. For ceramics, one would put such terms as *pearlware, creamware, Jackfield,* or *UID* (unidentified) *refined earthenware,* and so forth. For glass, a distinction should be made between curved and flat. For prehistoric ceramics, local type descriptions (e.g., Colington, Lamar, Weeden Island, etc.) could be used. For fasteners, the terms *spike, nail, tack,* or *staple* would be entered for this field.
Variety:	This would apply to specific clusters of attributes that distinguish a subtype. For example, Flow Blue is a particular variety of pearlware. For nails, *wrought, cut,* or *wire* would be entered.
Color:	Refers to the color of the artifact or its primary decoration. If a ceramic is plain, then nothing is entered. If it is a blue transfer-printed pearlware, then *blue* would be entered into this field. If it is a multicolored, hand-painted pearlware, then *polychrome* would be entered.
Element:	Refers to something other than a body fragment (i.e., rim, handle, base, etc.).
Decoration:	The primary decorative element characterizing the artifact. This would include such descriptions as "transfer-print," "painted," "fabric impressed," "simple stamped," and so on.
Dimensions:	This field is for measurements such as the diameter of buttons, length of projectile points, or bore diameter of pipe stems.
Remarks:	This field is for pertinent comments that don't necessarily fit in other fields. You could describe a maker's mark or note that the artifact is burned or that the type is similar to a specimen from another site.

Another advantage of computerized database systems is that you have the ability to quickly organize your entire assemblage on a variety of criteria. For example, you initially rough-sorted the artifacts on the basis of their composition. With a computerized database, you could print a summary table of your artifacts sorted by "Material." Or you could sort on the basis of provenience. This negates the advantage of waiting until you return from the field to assign catalog (FS) numbers. It wouldn't matter how they were assigned in the field since the computer could order them by excavation unit, or natural strata level, or component, or any context that made sense to the archaeologist.

One major fear that prevents many archaeologists from committing to a computerized system is the fear that their system will crash and they will lose all their data. Your system *will* crash at some point, just as the power in the lab will go out during a storm or your field vehicle will get a flat on some back road. Provisions can be made for dealing with system crashes just as they can be made to lessen the impact of any other emergency. Back up your data frequently, and have a printed hard copy as well.

Another legitimate fear that the lab manager has is that the database program selected will become obsolete. This *will* happen. It is important to look at the potential upgrade options for the program. In this case, it is probably wiser to go with a major commercial vendor with a large installed clientele rather than a small proprietary system. If a major vendor goes under, *someone* is likely to pick up the contract to service the former customers.

DATA ENTRY

The best way to make sure no data are lost is in the data entry phase of the artifact-cataloging process. It is important that the information be typed into the computer *exactly* the way the archaeologist desires. Computers do *exactly* what they are told. If you ask it find all the "shel-tempered" sherds in the database, it will find only those that were misspelled exactly in that fashion. So it is important that everyone using your database classifies the same artifact in the same way and that this information is carefully entered into the computer.

DATA ENCODING

If several archaeologists will be involved in the process of analysis, it is important that they agree on the artifact typology. This is the responsibility of the project director. She or he must ensure that everyone calls a particular piece of historic ceramic transfer-printed pearlware and not decorated refined earthenware or pearl-white ware with transfer-printed decoration or any other equally descriptive variant. A codebook available to all lab staff that describes different classes of artifacts and what the archaeologist should call them is essential.

DATA ENTRY SHEETS

Once the nomenclature is established, the data can be entered into the database structure. It is important that these data first be handwritten on separate sheets of paper with the different categories listed in columns (figure 9.5). This may seem like an extra, unnecessary step to individuals who are used to composing at the keyboard, yet there are very good reasons for doing so.

First, by sorting out the attributes on paper, the archaeologist gets a feel for how different artifacts should be classified and can check for consistency before the data are entered. Second, whereas a trained archaeologist must perform the actual artifact identification and analysis, anyone can type the data entry sheets into the computer. This is a useful task for students, who benefit by learning about artifact classification while relieving the archaeologist of the tedious time at the keyboard. Finally, and most important, these data entry sheets act as an emergency backup for your data should something go terribly wrong with your computer system.

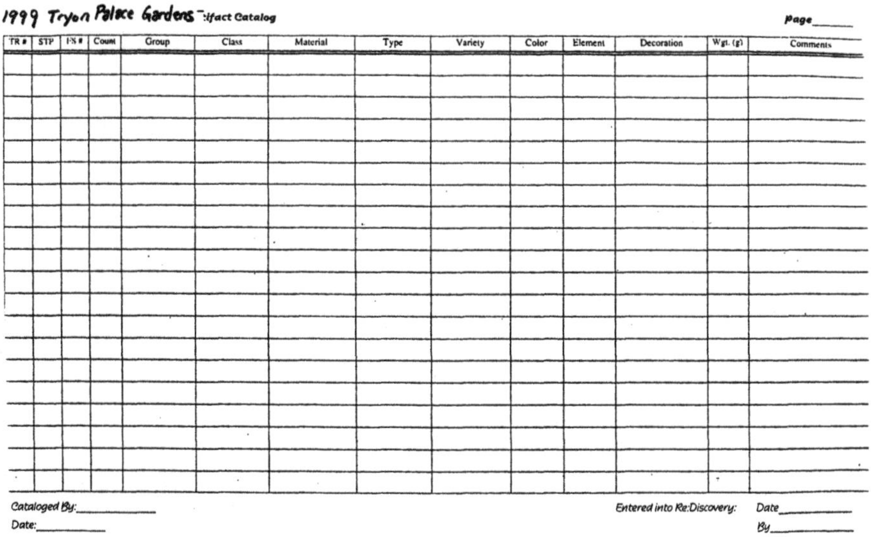
1999 Tryon Palace Gardens :ifact Catalog

Page______

TR #	STP	FS #	Count	Group	Class	Material	Type	Variety	Color	Element	Decoration	Wgt. (g)	Comments

Cataloged By:__________

Date:__________

Entered into Re:Discovery: Date__________

By__________

Figure 9.5 Data entry sheet. (Courtesy of the ECU Archaeology Lab.)

PROOFING HARD COPY

A final step for data entry applies whether you are using a computer, paper catalog sheets, or index cards to organize your collection. It is important that the archaeologists check and double-check their own work and that of their assistants. This is especially true of the data entered into a computerized system. The old (in computer time) adage "garbage in, garbage out" applies here. Once the data entry specialist has completed inputting the data, the database should be printed and scanned for misspellings and inconsistencies in classification. These anomalies should be corrected and a clean hard copy produced. The archaeologist is now ready to proceed to the next phase of artifact analysis.

10

DATA MANIPULATION

OBJECTIVES

The purpose of cataloging the artifacts is essentially to prepare the assemblage for more in-depth analysis. The purpose of this in-depth analysis or data manipulation is to aid the archaeologist in interpreting the artifact collection. So, in a sense, analysis is all about asking the right questions of your data and arranging the answers in a way that allows you to achieve the interpretive objectives of your research design.

STATISTICAL ANALYSES

A complete or even cursory examination of statistical analytic procedures is clearly beyond the scope of this book. However, it is important that the archaeologist understand what statistical analyses are and how they can be used and abused on archaeological data. A good introduction to the use of statistics in archaeology is David Hurst Thomas's *Refiguring Anthropology* (1986). Other good references exist (e.g., Drennan 1996). One such manual should be on every archaeologist's bookshelf.

Statistics are numbers. They are a numeric description of the archaeological data. The basic quantification procedures discussed in earlier chapters generate statistics. So, when archaeologists count and weigh the different categories of artifacts to be listed in a summary table, they are preparing statistical tables. This probably comes as something of a shock to the mathematically impaired student who sought refuge from statistics in the social sciences! Nearly every attribute of an artifact can be quantified. Counts and weights are obviously numeric data, but other aspects can be represented statistically. Artifact shapes and areas can be measured, colors can be recorded with a Munsell chroma scale (and even more accurately with computerized color sensors), and the volume of pots can be determined.

Statistics are also a tool to infer the characteristics of a data set that are missing or not directly observable. This type of statistical analysis, called *inferential statistics*, uses the procedures that are employed by the Harris and Gallup pollsters to predict the outcome of elections with only 2 percent of the voting precincts reporting in. Since archaeologists rarely have the opportunity to excavate an entire site, they must make inferences about the entire site based on the excavated portion. Inferential statistics offer ways of assessing the degree of confidence the archaeologist can have in conclusions regarding these extrapolations

SAMPLING

Making the sample of data collected as representative as possible of the entire site is the responsibility of the field archaeologist. However, often the data collected in the field are more than can be reasonably analyzed in the lab. This is especially true of many CRM projects whose time and budget constraints dictate the level of effort that can be expended on analysis. Budget limitations also limit the size of the collection that can be analyzed by a contracted specialist, such as a zooarchaeologist. Rather than send all the faunal remains to the zooarchaeologist a representative sample is culled from the total faunal assemblage. So what constitutes a "representative sample"?

There are basically two philosophies in devising a sampling strategy: judgmental and random. Judgmental sampling relies on the past experience or special knowledge of the archaeologist in compiling the sample. For example, if you wanted to know what kinds of animals were part of the diet of the Woodland component of your site, you might select the faunal remains from undisturbed feature contexts associated with Woodland ceramics rather than the remains found scattered in a mixed sheet midden.

Random sampling, on the other hand, is preferred when little is known about the archaeological collection or the archaeologist wants to eliminate any bias in the selection of the subsample. In this case, rather than choosing the fauna recovered from proveniences from a specific part of the site, the archaeologist might want to include all the animal bones from a couple of excavation units randomly chosen from the all those excavated.

Statistical analysis picks up where classification leaves off in determining the similarities and differences between artifact categories. Which attributes are related? Which never occur together? A judicious use of scatterplots can graphically depict relationships between artifact attributes that can also be expressed mathematically (i.e., as a linear regression formula). By revealing patterns in the data (e.g., glazing is correlated with historic ceramics), statistics can be used to generate hypotheses.

Statistical tests of probability, such as the Student's t, address the question "Is the correlation between these two attributes real or could their relationship be due to chance?" In this case, our research hypothesis would be that only historic ceramics are glazed. The null hypothesis, the one we wish to disprove, would state that there is no relationship between glazing and the time period in which ceramics were manufactured. One should note that since we are dealing with probabilities, you can never prove your research hypotheses; you merely fail to reject them. You should be wary of anyone who states that something has been "statistically proven"!

Statistical association should never be confused with what actually happened. That is, statistics can point to a connection, but the archaeologist must determine what that connection means. The statistical observation that glazing occurs only on historic ceramics is merely the impetus to ask the question "Why?" Performing the statistical analyses is one of the steps leading to the interpretation of your collection.

Archaeologists should never lose sight of why they are doing the statistical test in the first place. It is often easy to forget the big picture when immersed in a sea of attributes. As part of the shift to an explicitly scientific archaeology in the 1970s, archaeologists became obsessed with finding the most arcane statistical procedures imaginable. Papers weren't published unless they contained some statistical procedure no matter how irrelevant to the questions being asked. David Hurst Thomas, one of the leading proponents of statistical applications to archaeology, was so appalled at the abuse of these procedures that he wrote "The Awful Truth about Statistics in Archaeology" (1978), in which he was especially critical of the uncritical use of multivariate statistics. Fortunately, in most cases, he found that "the analysis is needlessly complex, so alien to anything remotely archaeological, that little harm is done" (Thomas 1978:240). He advocated a return to more elementary univariate or bivariate methods before jumping into the multivariate deep end. Since then, archaeology has undergone a humanistic paradigm shift, and statistics are more judiciously used. No matter what the prevailing school of thought, it is important to remember that statistics, like computers, are only means to an end, not an end in themselves.

PATTERNING

Archaeologists are always looking for patterns in their data. As discussed earlier, this is one of the primary reasons for the classification of artifacts. It is impossible to see any patterns or omissions in the data if they are in chaos. Patterns that interest the archaeologist can take many forms. They can refer to the pattern of the designs on ceramic vessels. They can refer to the regular arrangement of postmolds on a site. Sometimes, by grouping artifacts or their attributes into statistically significant categories, patterns are revealed that can tell much about the people who made the artifacts.

Albert Spaulding used a type of statistical test called a *cluster analysis* to determine which type of stylistic attributes were linked on ceramics of the Lower Mississippi Valley. He hoped to discover the patterns the makers of those pots thought were correct and so gain some insights into the thoughts of those prehistoric potters. Stanley South looked at the proportions of artifacts in different functional categories or their distribution across a site to gain some insight into the activities of the inhabitants of the sites he excavated.

SOUTH'S PATTERNS

Stanley South, like Thomas, felt that archaeologists could get so caught up in the methodology that they would miss the point of their efforts. He argued that solutions to archaeological problems do not come directly from the observations made on the data; they come from the archaeologist. To this end, he devised a number of empirical tests to help the archaeologist recognize patterns in the archaeological data that would provide a basis for the archaeological interpretation.

South's (1977:25) goal was to

demonstrate the patterned regularity of the archaeological record as well as the variability, under the belief that we can have no science without pattern recognition, and pattern cannot be refined without quantification. From pattern recognition, general empirical laws can be stated, and the explanation of why these laws are operative through the hypothetico-deductive process leads to theory building through testing hypotheses with new data.

Let's explore three of these pattern recognition processes.

The Brunswick Pattern (formulated from data recovered from excavations at Brunswick Town, North Carolina) of artifact disposal seems deceptively obvious. The pattern is simply that on British colonial sites of the eighteenth century, a concentrated refuse deposit will be found at the points of entrance and exit in dwellings, shops, and military fortifications. This is useful in determining the doorways for structures where only the foundation remains.

It would be short-sighted, however, to see this pattern as merely a tool to find the door to a structure. What does this pattern say about trash disposal patterns of the people of Brunswick Town? We don't just throw our refuse out the door. What sort of refuse was being disposed of out the door? Did other ethnic groups dispose of their refuse in like fashion? Did refuse disposal habits change through time? As can be seen, identifying a pattern serves as a point of departure for other studies.

While the Brunswick Pattern relies on careful attention to the spatial distribution of the artifact assemblage, the Carolina Pattern and the Frontier Pattern utilize an organizational approach derived by classifying artifacts from a number of eighteenth-century sites into eight functional categories. It essentially is a model pertaining to percentages of artifact categories that you would find on an eighteenth-century British colonial site. With the Carolina Pattern, those artifacts classified in the Kitchen functional group would predominate over those in the Architecture functional group, whereas the Frontier Pattern would reverse the importance of these two functional groups. These patterns are examples of how the manipulation of data can reveal patterns in an archaeological assemblage.

The method of organization of the data can reveal changes in an otherwise static artifact assemblage and vice versa. A good example of this can be seen in the data recovered from the sixteenth-century town of Puerto Real on the north coast of Haiti (Ewen 1991). When viewed chronologically by descriptive types (i.e., different varieties of majolicas and utilitarian wares), the assemblage greatly changed in both kind and number of artifacts during the course of the site's occupation. However, if these same artifacts were grouped functionally rather than stylistically (table 10.1), then the assemblage could be seen to change very little. The shifts in particular artifact types that were noted pertained to trends in style and fashion *within* the functional categories. The functional categories remained relatively stable through time, indicating that the pattern of colonial adaptation of the Spaniards changed very little through time at Puerto Real.

The versatile ceramic assemblage can be manipulated in a variety of ways to investigate a variety of questions. By examining stylistic motif and mineralogical composition, a sherd's point of origin can be determined and provide information regarding trade patterns. Predominance of vessel form can provide insights on food preparation and storage prac-

Table 10.1. Early versus Late Categories at Puerto Real			
Artifact Category		*Early*	*Late*
Majolica	#	1,400	7,682
	%	18.16	19.05
Hispanic Tablewares	#	139	1,513
	%	1.8	3.75
European Utilitarian Ceramics	#	1,963	10,870
	%	25.46	26.95
Non-Majolica European Tablewares	#	36	163
	%	.47	.40
Locally Made Ceramics	#	3,526	17,387
	%	45.73	43.11
Kitchen	#	232	1,037
	%	3.01	2.57
Structural Hardware	#	226	1,107
	%	2.93	2.74
Arms and Armor	#	8	15
	%	.10	.04
Clothing Related	#	116	297
	%	1.5	.74
Personal Items	#	24	169
	%	.31	.09
Activity	#	24	38
	%	.31	.42
Furniture Hardware	#	1	9
	%	.01	.02
Tools	#	2	18
	%	.03	.04
Toys and Games	#	2	9
	%	.03	.02
Harness and Tack	#	12	19
	%	.16	.05
TOTAL	#	7,711	40,333
	%	100	100

tices, which in turn can provoke questions concerning social interaction (e.g., do large vessels denote communal cooking or extended family residences?). Ceramics, as we have seen earlier, can also be used to examine patterns of status differentiation and folk classification systems.

CC INDEX

An archaeological assumption that has reached almost lawlike status is that the more exotic the ceramic, the higher the status of its owner. Thus, in prehistoric sites, individuals buried with highly decorated, imported vessels are usually interpreted as having more status than those buried with locally made plain wares. Similarly, on historic sites, structures associated with porcelain and other finely wrought imported wares are usually thought to have been occupied by individuals with higher status than those sites with locally made undecorated wares.

On historic sites of the eighteenth and nineteenth centuries, it is possible to classify the ceramic assemblage based on its relative value of the time, thanks to George Miller's (1980) CC (cream-colored ware) Index. The CC Index is an emic classification of ceramics based on decoration and price from contemporary commercial catalogs and shipping manifests, rather than the etically imposed ware types of the archaeologist. Those etic classifications, while good for dating and determining country of origin, are vulnerable to the subjective biases in classification (as anyone who has tried to distinguish a body sherd of late creamware from early pearlware can attest).

The CC Index can more easily and consistently classify pottery and answer questions about status and can be integrated with historical documents. It takes all cream-colored refined earthenwares and breaks them down into four categories: (1) undecorated, (2) minimal decoration (engine turned), (3) hand-painted, and (4) transfer print. These different categories are ranked according to their price when compared to the undecorated category, which has an index value of one. CC Indices are also scaled depending on the type of vessel form (i.e., plates, bowls, tea wares). Thus, the index reveals how much individuals were willing to spend on their tablewares. This may or may not be indicative of status but is certainly revealing of the individuals' choices and, perhaps, aspirations.

An example of how the CC Index can be used is its application to the ceramics assemblage from the Robert Hay house in New Bern, North Carolina. Hay was a carriage maker who plied his trade during the first half of the nineteenth century. Although his trade and financial records indicate that he was economically a member of the middle class, the historical record of the time suggests that he was considered in higher social status by the community. Late in life, he was forced to declare bankruptcy, allegedly because of debts incurred by his brother-in-law. The timely financial intervention of his upper-class friends saved him from complete ruin.

An analysis of the ceramic assemblage excavated at the Hay lot (Magoon 1998) revealed a much higher CC Index than expected for a working craftsman. This suggests that Robert Hay might have been living beyond his means to keep up with his society friends and that his deadbeat brother-in-law was merely the final straw that toppled his precarious fiscal situation. This example should serve notice that, as with all data manipulation, it is not the formula but how the results are interpreted in context that is important.

DATING

The concern with chronology has been one of the primary concerns of the archaeologist since the founding of the discipline. The Law of Superposition (strata on the bottom are older than the strata on top) is one of the few laws in archaeology. Chronometric techniques (discussed later) have allowed archaeologists to assign calendar dates to strata and features. These two dating strategies, the first providing a relative date, the second an absolute date, can be applied to artifacts as well.

SERIATION

One of the earliest means for determining which artifacts were older than others was the relative technique known as *seriation*. This technique arose under the Culture History paradigm when the construction of regional chronological frameworks was of paramount concern to the archaeologist. Seriation is a presumably temporal ordering of artifacts based on the assumption that certain attributes (e.g., stylistic motifs, technology, form, etc.) change at a regular rate and that the predominance of a particular attribute can be associated with a particular period in time.

For an excellent example of seriation in action, we can again return to the Lower Mississippi valley. James Ford (the protagonist in the

Ford–Spaulding debate) was interested in arranging the mostly single component sites in that region into chronological order. He recorded the percentages of the different ceramic types from a site on strips of paper. He then took these strips of paper and arranged them so that the percentages waxed and waned in popularity according to archaeological assumptions of how seriation works (figure 10.1). The assumptions guiding Ford's work in the Lower Mississippi Valley, that ceramic types evolved in a predictable manner, would be tested by historical archaeologists.

The idea of seriation seemed logical, but archaeologists lacking tight chronological control had never really tested the concept. James Deetz and Edwin Dethlefsen (1965) determined a way to test whether artifact attributes really did behave in a predictable manner by using

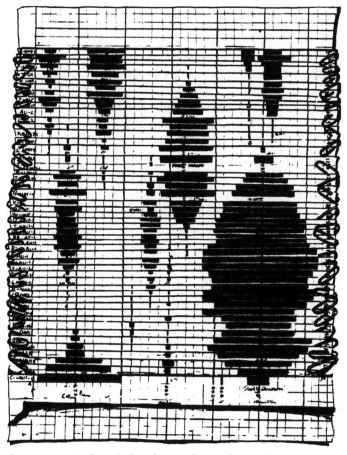

Figure 10.1　Ford's seriation chart. (After Ford 1952, figure 4.)

artifacts with stylistic attributes whose date was known: gravestones. They charted the occurrence of such different decorative motifs as death heads, cherubs, and urn and willows in several eighteenth-century cemeteries (figure 10.2). With the validity of the seriation concept established, archaeologists can note deviations from this pattern (e.g., the sudden disappearance of an attribute at its height of popularity) and investigate their causes.

DATING WITH HISTORIC ARTIFACTS

Often whole sites or individual strata are dated by using artifacts of a known age that they contain. This is similar to the paleontological dating practice of using marker fossils. Some historical artifacts and radiometrically dated prehistoric artifacts can be used in the same fashion. Historic artifacts are often used to establish a TPQ (*terminus post quem*) for an archaeological deposit.

Terminus post quem means the date *after* which the deposit was created. A simple example would be an undisturbed trash pit holding five coins dated 1920, 1921, 1924, 1925, and 1983. The TPQ for that deposit would be 1983. In other words, the trash pit could date no earlier than 1983, despite the dates on the other coins, since that is the earliest the 1983 coin could have been deposited. Archaeologists have determined TPQs for many varieties of historic ceramics, beads, and other artifacts whose date of manufacture is known.

The opposite of a TPQ is a *terminus ante quem* (TAQ), or date *before* which a deposit was created. The determination of the TAQ can be useful in establishing the end point of a certain activity. Returning to New Bern, we find recorded that a hurricane devastated the town in 1769. This event is clearly visible in the stratigraphic record as a thin layer of light-colored sand. When encountered, it establishes the TAQ of the deposits beneath it. Both TAQs and TPQs can be used in a number of ways to interpret the stratigraphy of a site.

The TPQs for various classes of artifacts have also been used statistically to determine the mean, median, and range of occupation dates for a site. This is often referred to as *formula dating*. One must keep in mind that these formulas do not yield precise dates, but simply get you in the ballpark or provoke further investigation. Your sample should at least consist of thirty specimens, and these formulas work best with collections from a relatively restricted time span.

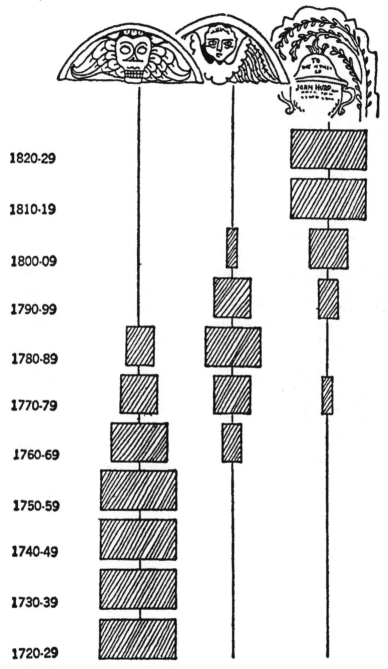

1820-29

1810-19

1800-09

1790-99

1780-89

1770-79

1760-69

1750-59

1740-49

1730-39

1720-29

Figure 10.2 Plot of tombstone seriation, Stoneham cemetery, Massachusetts. (From Deetz 1996; used by permission.)

PIPE STEMS

Tobacco pipes have long been used to date seventeenth- through nineteenth-century historic sites. The changing form of a pipe bowl is a distinctive attribute that can often provide a TPQ and date range for that artifact's use life (see Hume 1978:302–3). However, it is the pipe stem, or the bore diameter of the pipe stem to be more precise, that can be quantified and plugged into a formula that yields a rough date for the pipe stem assemblage. There are several methods of pipe stem dating.

J. C. "Pinky" Harrington was one of the first archaeologists to recognize that the bore hole of the clay pipe stem became narrower with the passage of time. The Harrington method (1954) is more like a seriation than a strictly formulaic approach to the dating of the pipe stems. The bore diameter of each of the pipe stem fragments in a collection would be measured by inserting a standard drill bit and recording the best fit. Drill bits made in increments of sixty-fourths of an inch became the de facto standard of measurement since they were handy and inexpensive. After all the pipe stems had been measured, an average bore diameter was calculated, which was then compared to a chart (figure 10.3). This placed the main occupation of the site within an approximate twenty-five-year period and worked surprisingly well.

Louis Binford (1969) hypothesized that the bore contracted at a constant rate and so derived a straight-line regression formula to arrive at a more precise date. According to Binford the mean date of a site's occupation could be calculated by the formula $y = 1931.85 - 38.26x$, where y = desired date and x = mean bore diameter of assemblage. The

1800 1750	77%	20%	3%			
1750 1710	13%	72%	15%			
1710 1680		12%	72%	16%		
1680 1650			18%	57%	25%	
1650 1620				21%	59%	20%
	4/64"	5/64"	6/64"	7/64"	8/64"	9/64"

Time period vs. pipe bore diameter

Figure 10.3   Harrington's pipe stem chart. (After Harrington 1954.)

date, 1931.85, was the date when the pipe stem would theoretically disappear given a constant rate of narrowing. The practical limitations of the formula is that the bore diameter levels out toward the end of the eighteenth century and doesn't work for dates after 1780.

In the statistical quest to build a better pipe stem formula, several archaeologists questioned whether the reduction in bore diameter was as regular as had been assumed. Based on the measurements of pipe stems from assemblages of known dates (see Hanson 1971), it was determined that a curvalinear regression better expressed the technological trend.

MEAN CERAMIC DATING

Another example of formula dating is the mean ceramic date formula. Developed by Stanley South (1977), it derives the mean date of occupation for a site. This formula relies on the archaeologist knowing the date range for the manufacture of specific artifact types.

$$Y = \frac{\sum\limits_{i=1}^{n} x_i f_i}{\sum\limits_{i=1}^{n} f_i} \qquad \begin{aligned} x_i &= \text{median} \\ f_i &= \text{sherd count} \end{aligned}$$

Let's say you excavated a sealed privy that had twenty-two sherds of plain creamware; fifty-three sherds of white, salt-glazed stoneware; eighteen sherds of Jackfield ware; and eighty-seven sherds of slipware. By consulting a chart of manufacture dates (e.g., South 1977:210–12), you can determine the median manufacture date (MMD) for each type of ceramic. From there it is a simple matter of multiplying the MMD by the number of sherds, totaling the products of all the types, and dividing that total by the total number of sherds (see table 10.2). The

Table 10.2. Mean Ceramic Date of Hypothetical Privy Feature

Type	Mean Manufacture Date	Number of Sherds	Total
Creamware	1791	22	39,402
WSG stoneware	1758	53	93,174
Jackfield ware	1760	18	31,680
Slipware	1733	87	150,771
		180	315,027

Mean ceramic date = 315,027(total)/180(total number of sherds) = 1750.15.

resulting mean ceramic date (MCD) of 1750.15 is the interpreted mid-point of use for the privy feature.

It is also possible, using the date ranges of the various ceramics and plotting them on a chart, to estimate the span of use visually (see South 1977:214–17). Many skeptics have decried the biases (e.g., the curation effect) that would potentially skew the resulting date. Yet, the formula does seem to work and can provide a ballpark figure in the absence of associated documentation.

SPATIAL ANALYSES

Once the chronological aspect of the artifact collection has been addressed, you can turn your attention to establishing the spatial relationships. *Spatial analysis* is the study of the placement of artifacts on a site. The Brunswick refuse disposal patterns discussed earlier comprise an example of the kind of information that spatial analyses can deliver. It is while performing spatial analyses that one can appreciate the importance of context and provenience. If the exact locations of the artifacts are not known, there can be no spatial analyses.

Spatial analyses can be performed on a number of levels, from intersite to intrasite and even within an activity area. Intersite analyses are the realm of settlement pattern studies and beyond the scope of this work. Looking at the patterns in the placement of artifacts begins at the intrasite site level. Within the site, the areas of interest can be further subdivided into the determination and analyses of communities (the maximum number of people who together occupy a settlement at any one period), neighborhoods (a group of households within a well-defined area), and households (artifact patterns believed to pertain to activities in a house).

The tighter the provenience control, the more focused the research questions can be. On some sites, where artifact counts are low, it is often advisable to piece plot each find. That is, rather than merely recording the excavation unit and level in which the artifact is located, the precise grid coordinates for the find are determined—a tedious field task that often pays off when the final maps are made by revealing activity areas. An activity area is an archaeological patterning of artifacts indicating a specific activity took place (lithic reduction, food preparation, etc.). With careful plotting, it is even possible to determine where the lithic craftsman sat as he manufactured tools by noting a clear area surrounded by a scattering of chert debitage.

ARTIFACT DENSITY

The differences in density of the distribution of artifacts across the surface of a site can also reveal the location of activity areas within a site. Subsurface testing (usually performed with shovels or power auger) is routinely used in CRM surveys to find sites and define their boundaries, usually on the basis of the presence or absence of artifacts within a shovel test. The plotting of the particular types of artifact found in the individual tests can reveal specific areas of interest within a site.

The site of Puerto Real was located when a collection of sixteenth-century Spanish artifacts was brought to the attention of archaeologists at the University of Florida. One of their first activities was to dig test pits at ten-meter intervals across the area to determine the site's boundaries. The site limits were determined, but much more was accomplished with the recovered data.

The analysis of these data was undertaken with the assistance of SYMAP, an early graphic program run on the university mainframe computer. The output from this program used different symbols and shading to denote concentrations of a specified artifact category. By noting the discrete clusters of stone and brick building debris, it was possible to define the location of individual structures within the site, though no above-ground traces remained (figure 10.4). By correlating these clusters of masonry with the types of ceramics found, archaeologists could also make predictions about the status of the occupants of these structures. Some of these predictions were later borne out in more extensive excavations (Williams 1986; Ewen 1991; Deagan 1995).

One of the most visually expressive ways to examine the distribution of the density of artifacts across a site is with a contour map. Contour maps are usually associated with topographic maps, which are simply graphic representations of landforms as indicated by differences in elevation. U.S. Geological Survey quadrangle maps have topographic information on them represented by contour lines.

Contour lines are a cartographic device used to indicate gradations in value. To prepare them, the x- and y-coordinates are plotted as locational data in two-dimensional space. The z-coordinate is the third value at a particular point. Elevation isn't the only information that can be portrayed by contour lines. When examining artifact distribution, it can also represent the quantity of artifacts (or a particular type of artifact) at a particular spot on a site. The density and distribution of artifacts across a site can be displayed graphically as a contour map.

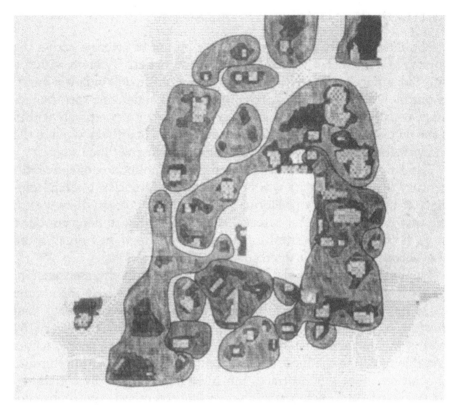

Figure 10.4   SYMAP of architectural debris at Puerto Real. (From Ewen 1991.)

The production of artifact density/distribution maps has been greatly facilitated by the increased use of personal computers. For example, Surfer (Golden Software) is an easy-to-use program that runs on desktop computers. It can quickly generate contour maps or a variety of other graphic representations (e.g., three-dimensional surface and chloropleth maps) for depicting density/distribution.

At the Governor Martin site, it was possible to produce a contour map of the density of burned clay daub with a map for the site. This was accomplished by totaling the weight of the daub found in each excavation unit. This became the z value, and the coordinates for the center of the excavation unit were used as the x and y values. The resulting map (figure 10.5) displays the distribution of daub and could be correlated with patterns of postmolds, suggesting that the structures of the Contact period Apalachee were of wattle and daub construction.

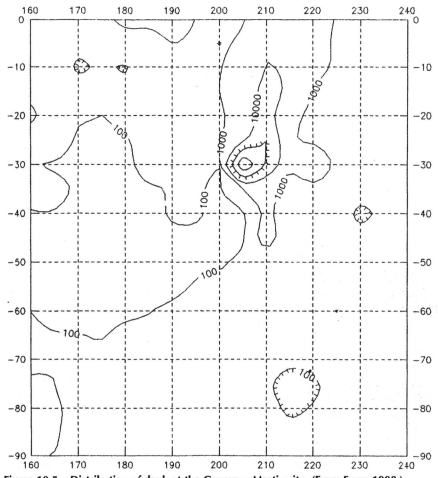

Figure 10.5   Distribution of daub at the Governor Martin site. (From Ewen 1998.)

REPLICATION

I often ask my students to question the epistemological assumptions of archaeology. How do we know what we think we know? Sharp-edged flint flakes are often called *scrapers*, but how do we know that that was their true purpose?

There are really only a few basic ways of inferring the purpose of archaeological features and artifacts. The first is the direct historical approach. Ethnographic accounts record that the earliest historic groups used an artifact in a specific way, so we infer that their prehistoric predecessors in the same area behaved in a like manner. This would constitute a sort of cultural uniformitarianism, if you will. Another way of knowing, ethnographic analogy, is bit more removed.

Ethnographic analogy posits that a prehistoric group probably behaved in a similar way to a known historic group possessing the same level of technology. This is how archaeologists can infer that Paleoindian peoples lived in egalitarian bands with few formal controls, by looking at modern groups of similar technical abilities and examining their lifestyles.

Archaeologists have analyzed modern tribal peoples in an effort to better understand the prehistoric cultures they study. This specialized branch of archaeology is called *ethnoarchaeology*. Archaeologists have actually excavated campsites of modern hunter-gatherers to see how observed behavior translates into preserved behavior. It has been possible to discover how certain tools could have been made, used, and discarded using an ethnoarchaeological approach.

A related approach to knowledge is the use of replication experiments in archaeology. This involves experimentation that attempts to recreate past conditions in an effort to gain an emic perspective on the past. It should be noted, however, that replicative experiments do not necessarily prove that an object was made or functioned in a particular way, merely that it was possible for it to have done so.

One of the questions that experimental archaeology attempts to answer is how certain artifacts were made or the effects of certain techniques on the manufacturing practice. For example, flint knapping is probably the most popular form of experimental archaeology. Individuals (e.g., Crabtree 1972) have experimented with different techniques of flake removal and shaping to gain greater insight into how lithic tools were made. Such replication experiments have demonstrated that heating chert makes it easier to work, thus providing a possible explanation for the presence of heat-treated chert on prehistoric sites.

Similarly, experiments have been conducted to determine the function of various artifacts. That is, it is one thing to say that flint hand cleavers could have been used to butcher mastodons during the Paleolithic, it is quite another to do it. Archaeologist George Frison actually butchered African elephants using only stone tools that he had made himself (Frison 1989). Did Paleoindian mastodon hunters cut up their prey in the same way? We may never know, but replication studies at least indicate what was possible and so eliminate certain blind alleys and allow the archaeologist to pursue answers in more productive areas.

11

SPECIALIZED ANALYSES

Many types of analyses require expensive equipment, special expertise, or other resources that are simply beyond the reach of most archaeological laboratories. Quite frankly, it is unrealistic for an independent archaeological contractor or small college laboratory to acquire a particle accelerator or amass a comparative collection of the mammals of North America when these resources exist elsewhere. It is a practical necessity to subcontract certain specialized analyses when they are required by your project. This section discusses some of these types of analyses and when they might be applicable.

CHRONOMETRIC DATING

One of the most commonly subcontracted specialized analyses is the chronometric dating of artifacts and ecofacts. There are several different methods for obtaining an absolute date for your sample, depending on the composition of your sample, the conditions of its deposition and recovery, and even the region of the world it is from. Each method has its own idiosyncrasies and limitations (table 11.1).

A couple of general rules of thumb apply to all methods of chronometric dating. Keep the handling of the specimen to a minimum. This lessens the chance of its contamination or alteration. Obtain as many samples as possible and submit multiple specimens for dating. If possible, use a couple of different methods. Dates obtained can vary widely, even within the same feature, so multiple specimens can help rule out an aberrant date.

Table 11.1. Chronometric Dating Methods		
Method	*Pros*	*Cons*
Dendrochronology	Extremely accurate.	Samples are relatively rare on sites. Sequence length varies from region to region.
Radiocarbon	Works on organic material. Reasonably accurate when calibrated; relatively inexpensive.	Must destroy much of the artifact to date it. Large confidence interval on some materials.
Accelerated mass spectrometry (AMS)	More accurate than conventional radiocarbon. Much smaller sample required.	More expensive than conventional radiocarbon.
Oxidized carbon ration (OCR)	Works on soil humates. Can serve as cross-reference for radiocarbon.	Few labs available. Date range not known at this time.
Thermoluminescence	Works on nonorganic material such as pottery and stone	Large confidence interval. Few commercial labs.
Obsidian hydration	Works on volcanic glass	Hydration varies from region to region and through time. Wide confidence interval. Few commercial labs.

DENDROCHRONOLOGY

Dendrochronology, or tree ring dating, is the oldest and most reliable absolute dating method available to the archaeologist. It was the only absolute method available to the archaeologist prior to 1950 and is used today to calibrate the more recently developed radiometric methods (discussed later). Dendrochronology was originally developed in the southwestern United States, where wood preservation was optimal, but recent work has established tree ring sequences in other parts of the country and the world (see the Laboratory of Tree-Ring Research at the University of Arizona at www.ltrr.arizona.edu, and the University of Arkansas Tree-Ring Laboratory at www.uark.edu/misc/dendro/). In historical archaeology, dendrochronology has been applied to standing wooden architecture to validate long-cherished dates for poorly documented historic structures. Often, as in the case of the Newbold-White house, formerly thought to be the oldest house in North Carolina, the structure turns out to be decades younger than previously thought!

The dendrochronology laboratory at the University of Arkansas recently determined that there was a prolonged drought in the Lower Mississippi Valley during the sixteenth century that may have had more to do with the depopulation of the area than any diseases introduced by the de Soto expedition (Burnett and Murray 1993). They also were able to determine that a drought existed along the mid-Atlantic coast at about the same time, which may also have been a contributing factor to the demise of the Lost Colony (Stahle et al. 1998).

RADIOCARBON

The discovery of the radiocarbon dating technique by Willard Libby in 1949 revolutionized archaeology. Prior to its discovery, the only method archaeologists had for attaching a calendar date to a site was dendrochronology, and its application was severely limited. Early use of radiocarbon dating was expensive, demanded large samples, and produced confidence ranges so broad as to be almost useless. However, lacking any alternative and seeing the tremendous potential of the method, archaeologists pursued the technique, refining it until it could reliably produce precise dates from small samples at a reasonable price (see ßeta Analytic at www.win.net/~analytic/ or Waikato Lab, New Zealand, at www.radiocarbondating.com).

Radiocarbon dating is a way of measuring how long an object has been dead. So any organic material can be dated, although some kinds (i.e., wood charcoal) produce better dates than others (shell is often hard to date). The procedure measures the decay rate of radioactive C14 into stable nitrogen. Organisms intake C14 and C12 while alive. When dead, the C14 starts to break down at a known rate. By measuring the difference between C14 and C12, you can determine how long the organism has been dead (for a more in-depth discussion of this procedure see www.radiocarbon.org/info/index.html).

It was discovered that when radiocarbon samples were checked against tree ring samples, the radiocarbon samples were in error even beyond the statistical confidence interval. It was determined the carbon level in the Earth's atmosphere had not remained constant over time, a key assumption in radiocarbon dating. Rather than abandon this dating method, archaeologists used the method that detected the error, dendrochronology, to correct it.

Thus, radiocarbon dates can be calibrated with a dendrochrono-logically derived scale to produce calendar dates as old as 60,000 B.P. These calibration programs are freely available over the Inter-net (e.g. OxCal at www.rlaha.ox.ac.uk/orau/index.htm or CALIB at depts.washington.edu/qil/dloadcalib/) and are also available in tab-ular form through the journal *Radiocarbon*.

One of the chief drawbacks of conventional radiocarbon dating is that it requires that you destroy a fairly large portion of your sample. This is not a problem when dealing with charcoal from a hearth fea-ture. However, when trying to date the parchment from the Dead Sea Scrolls or a bone fragment from Kennewick Man, every gram counts. Accelerator mass spectrometry dating is a method of radiocarbon dat-ing that actually counts the C14 atoms. This technique requires much smaller samples (<0.01grams) and produces more accurate re-sults. It costs more money but is usually worth the extra expense, and in some cases, it is the only acceptable alternative available.

The latest twist on the radiocarbon technique is the oxidizable car-bon ratio (OCR) dating. Based on the chemical analysis of charcoal within known environmental contexts, the OCR technique dates charcoal found in soil (Frink 1994:17). This technique works only on archaeological charcoal in a biochemically active, aerobic soil. This technique has been primarily used to reaffirm radiocarbon dates spanning the last eight thousand years. Its effective date range has not yet been determined, but the procedure is a promising addition to the archaeologist's dating repertoire.

THERMOLUMINESCENCE (TL)

TL dating is a widely known but not yet widely used method by North American archaeologists. This technique measures the amount of light energy released by a fired object (e.g., baked clay artifact) when it is heated rapidly so that it gives an indication of the time elapsed since the object was first fired (see Aitken 1985 for a more in-depth dis-cussion of how this procedure works). For example, it can be used to estimate the time that has passed since a pot was made to when it was subjected to the TL process. It has the advantage of working on a nonorganic material (e.g., ceramic and even chert) that is common on most archaeological sites and can date objects as old as 8000 B.P.

Unfortunately, TL has been plagued with accuracy problems so that it has, in the past, only reliably given a ballpark estimate of an object's age. For this reason, it has chiefly been used by museums to detect modern forgeries of ancient artifacts. Refinements of this technique continue and recent work on the prehistoric ceramics of the North Carolina coastal plain (Herbert 1997) show a good correlation between TL and radiocarbon dates.

Another, more pragmatic problem for the archaeologist is finding a lab that will perform the test. There are few commercial labs (e.g., Quaternary TL Surveys at www.users.globalnet.co.uk/~qtls/ and TOSL Research laboratory at www.dal.ca/~digs/t-intro.htm), like those that conduct radiocarbon dating. Many labs that do TL dating are usually dedicated to someone else's research and will only process other samples when convenient to their schedules.

OBSIDIAN HYDRATION

Another artifact dating technique that suffers from reliability problems is obsidian hydration. The basic premise here is that a fresh break on a piece of obsidian will absorb water from the atmosphere at a constant rate. The broken edge of an obsidian artifact can be examined under a microscope and the thickness of the hydration layer measured. Thus, it should be possible to be able to calculate the time that has passed since the last flakes were removed from the artifact.

There are a couple of limitations to obsidian hydration dating. First, the hydration rate varies with the composition of the obsidian. Second, the hydration rate also varies with the climate in different parts of the world, prompting one archaeologist (Ridings 1996) to question, "Where in the world *does* obsidian hydration dating work?" Still, the procedure is straightforward and inexpensive. So, if the limitations are kept in mind, obsidian hydration can be a useful tool for the archaeologist, especially when used in conjunction with other dating techniques.

FAUNAL

Faunal analysis, or the study of animal bones from archaeological sites is one of the most commonly performed types of specialized analysis. This is covered more in depth in another volume (see Toolkit, volume 5). However, it is important for the archaeologist to understand the types of questions that faunal analysis can answer and how this can be integrated with the artifact analysis.

It is a fairly common practice for contract archaeologists to send the faunal remains recovered on their projects off to a zooarchaeologist. The expectation of many archaeologists is that they will get a species list back from the specialist and maybe a comment or two about what the inhabitants of the site were eating. Therefore, it often comes as something of a shock when the zooarchaeologist responds that they need better provenience information, including the artifacts associated with each provenience and the archaeologist's preliminary interpretations of the site.

The context in which the bone was found is incredibly important to its interpretation. Whether the faunal remains were in a sealed trash pit, a hearth, accompanying human remains, or recovered from a coprolite affects how these bones will be viewed by the zooarchaeologist. Once the archaeologist becomes aware of the wealth of information faunal analysis can provide, the need for these data becomes readily apparent.

One of the basic interpretations that zooarchaeology can provide is dietary reconstruction. This transcends merely what was being eaten and includes the diversity and equitability (the variety and proportion of species being utilized as opposed to what was available), wild versus domestic species exploitation, the variability of the diet on an inter- and intrasite basis, and on historic sites, locally raised animals versus meat imported from out of the region. Knowing the animals being exploited by the sites' inhabitants can aid in the artifact analysis by correlating food items with their corresponding food preparation artifacts.

Zooarchaeological analysis is also helpful with the environmental reconstruction. What was the environment like around the site, how did it change through time, and what species were available for exploitation? The season of occupation of the site can also be determined by the species present in the assemblage. Some animal species (migratory waterfowl, anadromous fish, etc.) are only available in certain areas at certain times. This can be correlated with the artifact assemblage to give an idea of site function. For example, a North American site with projectile points, lithic debris, and Canada goose remains, might be interpreted as a fall hunting camp.

The domestication of certain species is revealed through changes in animal morphology (i.e., physical size, horn shape, etc.). The age and sex of the animal might reveal culling activity or breeding strategy. Again, correlated with the artifact assemblage (sheep shears, harness tack) a full picture of the animal exploitation activities at a site can be derived.

A fur trading post excavated in Wisconsin (Ewen 1986) presented an interpretive problem that was solved only after both the faunal and artifact assemblages had been analyzed and correlated with each other. Three cabins within the trading post stockade were known to have housed a high-status company partner and his family, a middle-status clerk, and several low-status employees. The initial matching of cabin with occupant had been on the basis of a cursory analysis of the artifacts associated with the cabins. The faunal analysis yielded results that were not in accord with the assumed status of the cabins' occupants. This prompted a reanalysis of the artifact and architectural data which suggested a different assignation for the cabin occupants that was more in line with the faunal data.

FLORAL

Many of the same questions (e.g., dietary reconstruction, seasonality, environmental reconstruction, etc.) that are addressed during zooarchaeological analysis can be examined with floral analysis as well. Floral analyses have more subspecialties. The specialties within ethnobotany include palynology, phytolith analysis, and wood/charcoal analysis.

Palynology, or pollen analysis, while not uncommon, is not widely used in archaeology because of the difficulty involved with collecting samples and the expense involved with the analysis. It has been used to give indications of plant domestication, though the results are usually suspect without corroborating archaeological or bioarchaeological evidence. However, it can be a very sensitive environmental indicator.

Pollen has been used to reconstruct past environment for archaeological sites in the arid west, where preservation is optimal. However, in the east, where preservation is poor and human disturbance is great, pollen analysis is used for other purposes such as detecting changes in land use over time. An analysis of an area known as Scottow's dock in Boston indicated that "ethnobotanical [pollen] data in urban situations are really waste-disposal or produce-loss patterns and reflect land use more accurately than they do diet" (Kelso and Beaudry 1990:78). In this case, the pollen record from the seventeenth through nineteenth centuries corroborates the documentary record as it traced lot use from commercial periphery (shipping dock) to residential back lot to use as a row of commercial shops.

Phytoliths are siliceous particles found with the stems and leaves of plants. They have a characteristic shape for each species of plant that allows the analyst to identify their presence even after the rest of the plant has long since decayed. Though the potential for phytoliths to inform archaeologists is widely recognized, this type of analysis is not widely used owing primarily to the intensive labor required in recovering and processing a sample and also the scarcity of specialists performing this service.

However, at Harper's Ferry, West Virginia, phytolith analysis was able to provide insight into landscaping activities at a private residence over time. This study (Rovner 1994) contradicted expectations of a lack of concern with yard appearance in an industrial community. Instead, it revealed an individual's kept yard that included flower and vegetable gardens. An examination of the documentary record shows that this period coincides with the use of the site as a boarding house, where a kitchen garden would have been useful, but not recorded.

Wood/charcoal analysis can have a direct bearing on artifact analysis. This type of analysis can determine the type of wood exploited for tool handles, building, or other purposes. An interesting project that availed itself of specialized charcoal analysis was the Hardman site in southwestern Arkansas (Early 1993). The artifact assemblage indicated that this site's inhabitants were involved in salt processing from the nearby saline springs. Water from these springs was boiled off in ceramic vessels, leaving the salt behind. The charcoal analysis indicated that hardwoods were the preferred heating material. Examination of documents describing the environment at the time of early settlement indicates that the forest around the Hardman site was primarily pine, while further away hardwoods predominated. Since pines are a primary reforestation species it was possible to get a good idea of the area being exploited for firewood by the prehistoric salt processors.

PETROGRAPHY

Petrographic analyses refer to those studies involving the identification of rocks and minerals. An examination of various lithic artifacts and ceramics can reveal such information as the source of the material from which the artifact is made, technological attributes pertaining to the manufacture of the artifact, and unusual inclusions that might characterize the composition of a particular artifact. This topic is included in the specialized analyses section in that petrographic analyses are often performed by geologists who have the expertise and equipment available for such analysis.

Petrographic analysis of ceramics and lithics goes beyond the simple macroscopic that an archaeologist routinely performs. For example, an archaeologist with a hand lens can usually determine the tempering agent of a ceramic without having to send the sherd to a specialist. A petrographic analysis would involve making a thin section of the sherd and viewing it under a microscope to identify and assess the proportions of the mineral inclusions in the clay. If samples of local clay sources were available, it would be possible to match the sherd to its source.

A more sophisticated and precise approach involves the use of a particle accelerator to determine the different types and proportions of elements in a specimen. PIXE analysis requires only a very small sample for a highly accurate reading that essentially eliminates observer bias. The problem with PIXE analysis, not unlike other special analyses requiring expensive equipment and trained personnel, is trying to find a lab that will perform the service.

The utility of petrographic analysis is not restricted to prehistoric applications. For example, it was possible using petrographic analysis to determine that the olive jar sherds found at the suspected site of Hernando de Soto's winter encampment in Tallahassee, Florida (Ewen and Hann 1998:76), originated in Spain rather than from a New World pottery. This helped strengthen the association of the site with the de Soto expedition, since olive jars commonly found on the later seventeenth-century Florida mission sites were primarily manufactured at New World potteries.

Lithic analysis can derive similar benefits from petrographic analysis. An archaeologist with a little training can usually determine the type of lithic material comprising the various tools in the lithic assemblage. The same archaeologist may even be able to tell the variety of stone (e.g., Mill Creek chert). However, this will not pin down a specific locality within a geological formation. Thus, to trace a tool to a specific quarry site, advanced petrographic analysis may be necessary.

I was once confronted with an interesting artifact that required the assistance of a geologist for positive identification. A local relic collector had found a large biface that appeared to be made out of glass. Curiously, the rest of the materials he had picked up in the area were chert pieces dating to the Late Archaic period. I was skeptical of the authenticity of the artifact since glass is an easily knapped material, and relic hunters often try to dupe the local professional archaeologist with recently made artifacts. Examination of the artifact by a geologist on the faculty, however, revealed the biface to be made from a remarkably pure quartz crystal (quartz is common to eastern North Carolina).

BIOARCHAEOLOGY

The final type of specialized analysis to be discussed here has the most to tell us about the people who made the artifacts we have examined thus far. Though artifacts are indirectly involved in this type of analysis, human bone can provide complementary data concerning the past biological and social environment. Bioarchaeology is the study of human skeletal remains in order to reconstruct past lifeways. The correlation of interpretations of the artifact assemblage with bioarchaeological data can result in new insights or correct previous assumptions.

Interpretations of past social behavior that one can gain from the analysis of human remains come from several analytical realms. Social stratification and belief systems can be gleaned from a study of mortuary patterns. By examining bone modifications, both naturally and culturally inflicted, it is possible to gain insight on kinds of injuries sustained, including repetitive motion and trauma. The bones can also reveal information concerning disease and nutrition. Broadening the view to many specimens can provide demographic information for a region or time period. But how does this relate to artifact analysis?

Bioarchaeological analysis, like other types of specialized analyses, complements the data recovered from the analysis of the artifact assemblage. For example, the patterning of artifacts from a slave cemetery in New York City might offer clues regarding the retention of African cultural practices (Blakey 1998). The accompanying bioarchaeological analysis reveals the general health of the individuals, the types of work they performed, and even how well they were eating.

Bioarchaeology has much to tell us about past populations, especially with the advent of such techniques as isotope and DNA analyses. These types of analyses are answering questions concerning when domesticates such as corn became a major part of the diet and degrees of relationship between past populations. The degree of relationship of excavated human remains to present Native American populations is a dominant theme in much of archaeology today.

The passage of the Native American Graves Protection and Repatriation Act (NAGPRA) in 1990 not only regulated the excavation of human remains on public lands but also compelled those repositories using federal funds or permits (virtually all of them) to inventory items they had in their care. The items to be accounted for include human remains, artifacts found in graves, sacred artifacts, and items of cultural patrimony. Following the inventory, the descendant populations are to be contacted and offered the opportunity to reclaim the skeletons and artifacts. Needless to say, this legislation has had a great impact on the field, not the least of which is that it has forced archaeologists to pay more attention to the care and storage of their collections.

12

 CURATION

One of the hidden shames of archaeology is the care (or lack thereof) accorded to artifacts after the analysis has been completed. While this subject is covered in more detail in volume 6 in this series, a few words are appropriate at this point, since the attention paid to the curation of a collection can have a direct bearing on any future analyses to be performed on the artifact collection.

Any archaeologist will testify to the importance of keeping good field notes and other records. Often the project archaeologist must rush to salvage a threatened site before conducting the analysis of the materials recovered from the last project. It is not unheard of for archaeologists at academic institutions to put off writing up the material recovered during their field schools for many seasons. In some archaeological consulting firms, the person who digs the site is not necessarily the person who writes the report.

It is good procedure to operate under the assumption that someone else will have to write up your fieldwork or that someone else will want to reanalyze your material. This means that you must ensure that all your artifacts and field and lab records are properly curated so that reanalysis is possible. There is no substitute for having dug the site yourself, but with the artifacts adequately documented and stored, the person that follows you should be able to reconstruct your fieldwork and draw valid conclusions from the data.

ARTIFACTS

Artifacts should be cleaned and labeled as to their provenience and stored in plastic zip-top bags. Paper bags deteriorate over time and have a tendency to split open when pulled for reanalysis. The provenience information should be printed on a card and stored inside the plastic bag rather than written on the bag itself with a permanent marker. The markers are *not* permanent, and the ink flakes off over time.

The purpose of packaging is to preserve the artifacts for future research. Bags of artifacts should be stored in acid-free cardboard or plastic containers. Artifacts susceptible to moisture damage should have packets of silica gel included in the storage container. If the collection has been sorted, then there should be documentation for the basis of the sorting included in the artifact box. Don't overpack the boxes—this damages the artifacts and makes the boxes difficult to handle.

Care should also be extended to preventing vermin from destroying artifacts or the bags that hold them. Returning from Haiti with a season's worth of artifacts, we were compelled to seal them in a room and fumigate them before they would be admitted to the United States. This was a wise move on the part of the customs officials as we found that an amazing collection of insects had infiltrated the cardboard boxes during shipping as well as a small colony of bats! A colleague related that mice infiltrated the plastic box and bags in which his artifacts were packaged in order to get at the paper provenience tags. These cautionary tales apply to the accompanying archaeological project documentation as well.

PROJECT RECORDS

All project records should be assembled and stored together. The paranoid collections manager (and this is a good trait!) may want to make duplicate records and store them in a separate location. The project field records include the field notes, photographs and slides, provenience catalog, and excavation forms for units and features. The lab records will include documentation concerning the level of processing, artifact inventory sheets, and any comments concerning the conservation needs of the artifacts. Reference as to the location of these documents should be attached to the artifact boxes and vice versa. Artifacts without their documentation have lost much of their archaeological significance.

PART IV

FINAL THOUGHTS

This section reiterates the purpose of the book—to get the readers to stop and consider why they are employing different analytical techniques—and then speculates on future trends in artifact analysis. Clearly technology, especially evolving computer applications, will play an ever-increasing role in artifact analysis. The main benefit of this technology is the ability it gives the archaeologist to ask increasingly complex questions of increasingly larger data sets. This is particularly important for the contract archaeologist working under a deadline. Another benefit of this increasingly powerful (and affordable) technology is the ability to analyze and record an artifact through digital imagery. This allows the archaeologist to gain more information with less handling of fragile artifacts. Enhanced information exchange via the Internet will allow colleagues to consult and publish in a timely manner.

This book concludes on the note that you will, in all probability, not be the last one to look at the data you've unearthed. We may not be able to predict all the new questions that will be asked of the data, but we can be assured that new ones will be asked and our knowledge of the past will continue to advance.

13

 **CONCLUSION**

This text is not intended to be a blueprint of the "right" way to conduct artifact analysis. The right way is the way that addresses the questions posed in the archaeological research design. Different questions require different types of analyses. Thus, to provide a complete "how to" book, perhaps in the Artifact Analysis for Dummies series, would require more pages than *Windows XP for Dummies* and still would not cover all contingencies. So what good is this volume?

The purpose of this volume, to reiterate the introduction, is to understand the goals of artifact analysis. It is only after those goals are defined, that the archaeologist can begin to formulate a plan to achieve them. The basic steps of artifact analysis—identification, classification, quantification, manipulation, and interpretation—have all been discussed and examples of how some archaeologists have approached these procedures were discussed.

The examples of artifact analyses provided in this text were just that, examples of analytic procedures, meant to give the reader an idea of the techniques that some archaeologists have employed. As I caution my graduate students when they go to work for another archaeologist, "If you are asked to perform a task differently than the way you were taught, don't tell your supervisors that they are doing it wrong! Learn the new way, and then, when you run your own project, you can select the way that works best for you." So it is with this text. If it gets the reader to stop and consider why they are performing different analytical procedures, then it will have served its purpose.

FUTURE DIRECTIONS

This chapter is fraught with peril. What are the future directions in artifact analysis—same old same old, or bold new innovations? Probably both statements are true to a certain extent. Some general predictions are easy. Computers will continue to play an ever-increasing role in the archaeological laboratory. The specific predictions are harder. Which computer platform will prevail? Which computer programs will be the standards? When I received my doctorate, WordStar, Visicalc, and dBase were the standards for word processing, spreadsheets, and database applications. At this writing, those programs either have been surpassed by competitors or no longer even exist.

Predicting what questions artifact analysis will be addressing is difficult as well. Archaeology is about due for another minor paradigm shift. The postprocessual paradigm has been around for nearly twenty years, which is about the life span of a theoretical cycle. Since the artifact analysis is geared to the kinds of questions being asked, the new millennium may be ushering in new theoretical approaches as well.

MORE POWERFUL COMPUTER APPLICATIONS

There is no doubt that the increased use of more powerful computers and software applications will be the rule in various types of archaeological analysis. Database queries that took an hour or more to run ten years ago take a matter of minutes or even seconds today. However, time savings is not the big payoff from this new technology. The principal benefit is the ability to address more and more complex questions of larger and larger data sets. Questions that would not even have been considered years ago because of the time requirements can now be asked by even novice archaeologists.

The wonders of computers have been extolled throughout this text, and, while they are a great help to the archaeologist, it should always be remembered that they are only tools. The computer is only as good as the archaeologist that uses it. If the archaeologist does not understand the basic principles of statistics, then even a Cray supercomputer will not be of much assistance. Computers will not do your analysis for you, they *will* help you analyze artifacts more efficiently by performing the tedious calculations or sorting through the reams of data required by your analyses. Better computers simply allow you to concentrate on asking better questions.

LARGE DATA SETS

Probably the biggest impact of the computer for the archaeologist is the enhanced access to large data sets. As the storage capacity of desktop computers increases, so does the ability to do complex comparisons of data within large sites and even between sites. Once all the data from all the sites that a lab has excavated have been entered into a computerized database, anyone can find out every site that has yielded a particular type of pottery. It is not necessary to go through every box of artifacts or track down the individual archaeologists that worked on all those sites and then rely on their memories.

NETWORKED DATABASES

Why should your queries be restricted to your lab? Networking technology makes it possible for computers to link to one another either directly or over the Internet. The federal government and many state agencies are assembling archaeological data and making it available online. The National Archaeological Database (NADB), mentioned earlier, that is maintained for the National Park Service aims to eventually have all archaeological site data for the country in a single huge database that can be accessed over the Internet.

Two big hurdles hinder the compilation of these huge archaeological databases, and neither of them involves computer hardware. The first is one that has already been discussed and that is trying to forge some sort of compatibility between existing databases. Finding a database structure that meets every archaeologist's needs may prove as elusive as the Lost Colony.

The second problem stems from the first. Even if a common data structure can be agreed on, if existing databases cannot be made to be compatible, then we are looking at a massive data reentry project. I have no doubt that this will take place in the future. Like the massive NAGPRA inventory effort, it will slowly happen, laboratory by laboratory.

THE INTERNET

Access to databases is not the only role that the Internet will play in artifact analysis. The information highway also allows archaeologists to consult with each other. Rather than waiting for a conference to query your colleagues, you can contact them electronically, send them text and graphics, and have a reply the same day. At least the technology exists to do so; whether your colleagues are quick to respond is an uncontrolled variable.

DISCUSSION GROUPS

There are a number of email discussion groups (table 13.1) to which an archaeologist can subscribe. Most of these listserves have a theme

Table 13.1. Archaeology on the Internet

Discussion Groups

ArchNet Forum	General discussion	http://archnet.org/forum/view.tcl?message_id=28
ACRA-L	CRM issues	Send email message subscribe acra-l "your name" to Listproc@listproc.nonprofit.net
ARCH-L	General discussion	Send email message subscribe arch-l "your name" to Listserve@listserve.tamu.edu

Gateways

ArchNet	http://archnet.org/lobby.tcl
Archaeology on the Net	www.serve.com/archaeology/ring/index.html
About.com's Archaeology	http://archaeology.miningco.com/science/archaeology/index.htm
The Archaeology Channel	http://www.archaeologychannel.org
Anthropology Resources on the Internet	http:www.aaanet.org/resinet.htm

E-Journals

Internet Archaeology	http://interarch.ac.uk/
Archaeology Magazine	http://www.archaeology.org/
Journal of Archaeological Research	http://www.wkap.nl/jrnltoc.htm/1059-0161
E-tiquity	http://e-tiquity.saa.org

Archaeological Sites

Queen Anne's Revenge	http://www.ah.dcr.state.nc.us/qar/default.htm
Cahokia Mounds	http://medicine.wustl.edu/~mckinney/cahokia/cahokia.html
Jamestown	http://www.apva.org

Alternative Archaeology

Quest for the Lost Civilization	http://members.aol.com/thelogo/quest
Earth/matriX	http://www.earthmatrix.com/home.html

(e.g., historical archaeology, classical archaeology, etc.) around which threaded discussions take place. If an archaeologist has a particularly hard to identify artifact or wants to know whether anyone else has ever recovered a certain type of ceramic, this information can be gathered by posting a request on the list and waiting for the responses. These lists can also provide a forum for the discussion of various theoretical approaches, analytical techniques, and the occasional flame war (i.e., an on-line heated exchange) between individuals with different opinions.

WORLD WIDE WEB

A component of the Internet is the World Wide Web. The web is especially useful for archaeologists in that it is a graphic environment. Many organizations (see table 13.1) have home pages that provide a great deal information about their activities and membership. Some organizations, such as the Society for American Archaeology, have gone so far as to discontinue printing their newsletter and instead post it electronically on their home page. Most archaeological journals either are publishing on the web in some form or have plans to do so.

Individual projects (table 13.1) have their own web pages where you can see pictures of their excavations and the artifacts that have been recovered. There are usually e-mail links to the project staff that allow the web page visitors to contact the project archaeologists directly with their questions.

Increased use of the web by archaeologists in the future seems assured. Personal webpages are becoming common and several e-zines or journals being published on the web are already happening. This has caused concern among many archaeologists about the quality of the material being posted on the web. The fear is that many people will potentially make uncritical use of unreliable data. This is a valid concern. Many class reports I receive have clearly been downloaded from the web, thus replacing the *Encyclopaedia Britannica* as the chief source of information for incoming freshmen. The only response at this point is caveat emptor: Let the user beware! Treat the web resource the same way as an unrefereed site report or a book published by a vanity press.

DIGITAL RENDERING OF ARTIFACTS

Archaeology is benefiting (as it always has) from innovations developed for other disciplines. One way that this pertains to the physical analysis of artifacts is by using computers to digitally reconstruct an artifact from its fragments.

RESIN CASTING

Archaeologists have long taken advantage of nearby hospitals to X-ray important finds that are heavily corroded or covered with incrustations of sediment. At the Governor Martin site in Tallahassee, a corroded mass of iron oxide was X-rayed to reveal a patch of chain mail armor. This allowed the archaeologists to confirm the function of the myriad single links found elsewhere on the site (Ewen 1989:38). Underwater archaeologists routinely X-ray coral-encrusted objects found on shipwreck sites since these often contain artifacts within the concretions.

New technologies have taken the X-ray technique to the next level. An artifact can be sent through a CAT scanner that produces an image of both the artifact's surface and interior. This procedure has been used to great effect in the study of Egyptian mummies since it allows the archaeologist to examine the body without unwrapping it.

Innova International, a company that primarily deals with medical clients, has combined the use of CT scanners with an advanced resin-casting technology to produce replicas of artifacts without any damage to the artifact. It is possible to isolate different parts of the artifact and reproduce each of those parts in a different-colored resin. For example, a spear point embedded in a bone can be cast in a dark resin while the bone itself is reproduced in a clear resin. Once the rendering is complete, the artifact reproduction can be examined without further handling of the original.

DIGITAL IMAGING ANALYSIS

As previously discussed, digital imaging software such as Photoshop or AutoCAD can be used to perform many metric analyses on images of an artifact so that the physical artifact need never be handled. A three-dimensional image of the artifact can be produced, and, if one dimension is known, virtually every other dimension can be calculated or extrapolated with a speed and accuracy surpassing those obtained by most lab technicians using conventional measuring devices. These images can be retained for further study should the actual artifact be removed from the laboratory.

IMPACT OF NAGPRA

The possibility that many artifacts and human remains could be repatriated has greatly impacted the way certain analyses are and will be conducted in the future. The Native American Grave Protection and Repatriation Act, besides dealing with the disposition of archaeologically recovered human remains, specifies that artifacts identified as grave goods, ceremonial items, or items of cultural patrimony be repatriated to their cultural descendants. This has introduced a new classificatory criterion for an archaeological assemblage: potential eligibility for repatriation.

Though the thought of relinquishing control of material recovered from an archaeological project disturbs some archaeologists, NAGPRA has brought many benefits. Artifact collections are analyzed more expeditiously when the threat of their return is imminent. The Native American community has become more involved with archaeologists and their analytic techniques. This in turn has encouraged an emic perspective to be considered by even the most hardened processual archaeologist. It has also fostered a greater respect and concern for archaeological remains, and so more attention has been paid to their curation and the possibilities of future analyses.

The development of some of the noninvasive analytical techniques discussed earlier was inspired or at least welcomed by those archaeologists dealing with repatriatable remains. The ability to analyze a bone or artifact without destroying a piece of it is usually important in such cases. Also important is the ability to have an enhanced graphic representation of the artifact should the artifact itself be returned. However, archaeologists must be cautioned that some Native groups are unhappy with even representations or replicas of ceremonial items being used outside of their sacred contexts.

REANALYSIS OF ARCHIVED COLLECTIONS

The final obvious trend for future artifact analyses is the analysis of previously excavated collections. In many cases, these collections have never undergone formal analysis. Many large excavation projects were conducted during the Great Depression under the auspices of the Works Progress Administration or the Civilian Conservation Corps. Funding was expended primarily during the field phase, which often employed hundreds of workers. Unfortunately, the same level of funding was not available for the analysis of the mountains of data recovered and so many of these collections were only partially analyzed or not analyzed at all.

An example of this legacy (Lyon 1996:207–8) demonstrates both the research potential of these collections and the importance of keeping good field records. Archaeologist Chester DePratter took on the task of finishing the final reports on excavations in Chatham County, Georgia, that had taken place from 1938 to 1942. His work was hindered by the fact that most of the site excavation maps were missing, and the artifacts were in some disarray after half a century of being shuttled from repository to repository. Still, the report was finished and the data were finally available in published form rather than as anecdotal memories of a vanishing generation of archaeologists.

Even collections that have been fully analyzed and published can often benefit from reanalysis. Times, and the questions being asked, change. New analytical techniques (e.g., PIXE analysis of ceramics, DNA extraction from bone) provoke new questions or the questioning of old answers. Questions concerning the gender roles of a site's inhabitants may not have seemed important a generation ago and yet are the focus of much current research.

The archaeologist can anticipate the needs of future archaeologists by publishing their work. This includes the methods and results of their analyses so that their efforts need not be duplicated. They must also ensure the availability of these data by preserving the artifact collection with sound curatorial procedures. The exact kinds of questions that will be asked of the artifact assemblage in the future are difficult to predict, except that some will be different and will require new and innovative analytical procedures.

CONCLUSION

I started this book with an Indiana Jones analogy, so it is appropriate that I end with another. At the climax of the movie *Indiana Jones and the Last Crusade*, Dr. Jones and a Nazi rival are confronted with a typological dilemma: Which of the dozens of cups in a given assemblage is the Holy Grail? The evil scientist hypothesizes that, since Christ was a person of importance to the world, the cup would be the most ornate and costly of the collection. To test this hypothesis, he fills the cup he has chosen with water and drinks from it. If his hypothesis is correct, he could expect to receive immortality. Instead, he dies a particularly gruesome death, thus disproving his hypothesis. The Guardian of the Grail turns to Jones and dead-pans, "He chose poorly." Jones, with this additional information, revises the hypothesis, makes the correct selection, and lives to make another sequel.

Archaeologists classify their artifacts, make assumptions about their makers, and test their hypotheses all the time. Fortunately, the consequences of incorrect interpretations are less dire than this example. Quite the opposite, in fact—disproving incorrect hypotheses can be as rewarding, from a knowledge-gained standpoint, as corroborating a cherished hypothesis. Either way, you have learned something about the past, which is the whole point of archaeology, after all.

 **REFERENCES**

Adovasio, J. M.
  1977 *Basketry Technology: A Guide to Identification and Analysis.* Aldine Manuals on Archaeology. Aldine, Chicago.

Aitken, M.
  1985 *Thermoluminescence Dating.* Academic Press, New York.

Ashmore, W., and R. J. Sharer
  1996 *Discovering Our Past,* 2d ed. Mayfield, Mountain View, California.

Barnes, James and Kathleen Cande
  1994 *Laboratory Procedures.* Sponsored Research Program. Arkansas Archeological Survey, Fayetteville.

Bauman, R.
  1968 Glass and Glasswares. In *Handbook for Historical Archaeology,* J. Cotter (ed.), vol. 1, pp. 30–36. Society for Historical Archaeology, Wyncote, Pennsylvania.

Beaudry, M. C., J. Long, H. M. Miller, F. D. Neiman, and G. W. Stone
  1983 A Vessel Typology for Early Chesapeake Ceramics: The Potomac Typology System. *Historical Archaeology* 17(1):18–43.

Binford, L. R.
  1969 A New Method of Calculating Dates from Kaolin Pipe Stem Samples. *Southeastern Archaeological Conference Newsletter* 9(1):19–21.

Blakey, Michael L.
  1998 The New York African Burial Ground Project: An Examination of Enslaved Lives, a Construction of Ancestral Ties. *Transforming Anthropology* 7(1):53–58.

Brauner, D. (ed.)
    2000   *Approaches to Material Culture Research for Historical Ar-
            chaeologists*, 2d ed. Society for Historical Archaeology, Califor-
            nia, Pennsylvania.

Brown, M. L.
    1980   *Firearms in Colonial America: The Impact of History and Tech-
            nology 1492–1792*. Smithsonian Institution Press, Washington,
            D.C.

Burnett, B. A., and K. A. Murray
    1993   Death, Drought, and de Soto: The Bioarcheology of Depopula-
            tion. In *The Expedition of Hernando de Soto West of the Mis-
            sissippi, 1541–1543*, G. Young and M. P. Hoffman (eds.), pp.
            227–36. University of Arkansas Press, Fayetteville.

Busch, J.
    1981   An Introduction to the Tin Can. *Historical Archaeology*
            15(1):95–104.

Cabak, M., M. Groover, and M. Inkrot
    1999   Rural Modernization during the Recent Past: Farmstead Ar-
            chaeology in the Aiken Plateau. *Historical Archaeology*
            33(4):19–43.

Callahan, E.
    1990   The Basics of Biface Knapping in the Eastern Fluted Point Tra-
            dition: A Manual for Flintknappers and Lithic Analysts. *Ar-
            chaeology of Eastern North America* 7:1–180.

Carr, P. (ed.)
    1994   *The Organization of North American Prehistoric Chipped
            Stone Tool Technologies*. Archaeology Series 7. International
            Monographs in Prehistory, Ann Arbor, Michigan.

Clifton, R. P.
    1970   *Barbs, Prongs, Points, Prickers, and Stickers: A Complete and
            Illustrated Catalog of Antique Barbed Wire*. University of Ok-
            lahoma Press, Norman.

Collins, M.
    1975   Lithic Technology as a Means of Processual Inference. In *Mak-
            ing and Using Stone Tools*, E. Swanson (ed.). Mouton, Paris.

Crabtree, D. E.
    1972   *An Introduction to Flintworking*. Occasional Papers of the
            Idaho Museum of Natural History 28. Idaho Museum of Natural
            History, Boise.

Davis, R. P. S., Jr., P. Livingood, H. T. Ward, and V. Steponitis
    1998   *Excavating Occaneechi Town: Archaeology of an Eighteenth-Century Indian Village in North Carolina*. University of North Carolina Press, Chapel Hill.

Deagan, K. A.
    1983   *Spanish St. Augustine: The Archaeology of a Creole Community*. Academic Press, New York.

Deagan, K. A.
    1987   *Artifacts of the Spanish Colonies of Florida and the Caribbean 1500–1800*. Vol. 1: Ceramics, Glassware, and Beads. Smithsonian Institution Press, Washington, D.C.

Deagan, K. A. (ed.)
    1995   *Puerto Real: The Archaeology of a Sixteenth-Century Spanish Town in Hispaniola*. University Press of Florida, Gainesville.

Deetz, J.
    1996   *In Small Things Forgotten*. Anchor Books/Doubleday, New York.

Deetz, J., and E. Dethlefsen
    1965   The Doppler Effect and Archaeology: A Consideration of the Spatial Aspects of Seriation. *Southwestern Journal of Anthropology* 21(3):196–206.

Demmy, G.
    1967   A Progress Report on: Glass Dating, An Archaeologist's Evaluation of the Concept. *Historical Archaeology* 1:49–51.

Diagram Group
    1980   *Weapons: An International Encyclopedia from 5000 BC to 2000 AD*. St. Martin's Press, New York.

Domanski, M., and J. A. Webb
    1992   Effect of Heat Treatment on Siliceous Rocks Used in Prehistoric Lithic Technology. *Journal of Field Archaeology* 19:601–14.

Dowman, E.
    1970   *Conservation in Field Archaeology*. Methuen, London.

Drennan, R. D.
    1996   *Statistics for the Archaeologist: A Common Sense Approach*. Interdisciplinary Contributions to Archaeology. Plenum Press, New York.

Early, A.
    1993   *Caddoan Saltmakers in the Ouachita Valley*. Research Series 43. Arkansas Archeological Survey, Fayetteville.

Edwards, J. P., and T. Wells
1994 *Historic Louisiana Nails: Aids to the Dating of Old Buildings.* Fred B. Kniffen Cultural Resources Laboratory Monograph Series 2. Louisiana State University, Baton Rouge.

Ewen, C. R.
1986 Fur Trade Zooarchaeology: A Study of Frontier Hierarchies. *Historical Archaeology* 20(1):15–28.
1989 Apalachee Winter. *Archaeology* 42(3):37–41.
1991 *From Spaniard to Creole.* University of Alabama Press, Tuscaloosa.
1995 Historic Homesteads: To Dig or Not to Dig. Paper presented at the 52d Annual Southeastern Archaeological Conference, Knoxville, Tennessee.
1996 Continuity and Change: De Soto and the Apalachee. *Historical Archaeology* 30(2):41–53.

Ewen, C. R., and J. H. Hann
1998 *Hernando de Soto among the Apalachee: The Archaeology of the First Winter Encampment.* University Press of Florida, Gainesville.

Fagan, B. M.
1997 *In the Beginning.* 9th ed. Addison Wesley Longman, New York.

Feder, K. L.
1996 *Frauds, Myths, and Mysteries.* Mayfield, Mountain View, California.

Fike, R. E.
1987 *The Bottle Book: A Comprehensive Guide to Historic, Embossed Medicine Bottles.* Peregrine Smith Books, Salt Lake City.

Flenniken, J.
1984 The Past, Present and Future of Flintknapping: An Anthropological Perspective. *Annual Review of Anthropology* 13: 187–203.

Flenniken, J., and E. Garrison
1975 Thermally Altered Novaculite and Stone Tool Manufacturing Techniques. *Journal of Field Archaeology* 2:125–32.

Fontana, B. L.
1978 On the Meaning of Historic Sites Archaeology. In *Historical Archaeology: A Guide to the Substantive and Theoretical Contributions*, R. L. Schuyler (ed.), pp. 23–26. Baywood, Farmingdale, New York.

Ford, J. A.
1954 The Type Concept Revisited. *American Anthropologist* 56(1): 42–54.
1972 *A Quantitative Method for Deriving Cultural Chronology.* Reprint of 1962 edition ed. Museum Brief 9. Museum of Anthropology, University of Missouri, Columbia.

Frink, D. S.
1994 The Oxidizable Carbon Ratio (OCR): A Proposed Solution to Some of the Problems Encountered with Radiocarbon Data. *North American Archaeologist* 15(1):17–29.

Frison, G.
1989 Experimental Use of Clovis Weaponry and Tools on African Elephants. *American Antiquity* 54(4):766–84.

Hamilton, T. M.
1968 *Early Indian Trade Guns: 1625–1775.* Contributions of the Museum of the Great Plains 3. Museum of the Great Plains, Lawton, Oklahoma.

Hanson, L. H.
1971 Kaolin Pipe Stems—Boring in on a Fallacy. *Conference on Historic Sites Archaeology Papers* 4(1):2–15.

Harrington, J. C.
1954 Dating Stem Fragments of Seventeenth and Eighteenth Century Clay Tobacco Pipes. *Quarterly Bulletin of the Archaeological Society of Virginia* 9(1):9–13.

Henry, D. O., and G. H. Odell (eds.)
1989 *Alternative Approaches to Lithic Analysis.* 1. American Anthropological Association, Washington D.C.

Herbert, J. M.
1997 *Refining Prehistoric Culture Chronology in Southern Coastal North Carolina: Pottery from the Papanow and Pond Trail Sites.* Research Laboratories of Anthropology. University of North Carolina, Chapel Hill.

Herbert, J. M.
1999 Introduction to "Prehistoric Pottery: Series and Sequence on the Carolina Coast." *North Carolina Archaeology* 48:1–2

Hester, T., H. Shafer, and F. Feder
1997 *Field Methods in Archaeology.* 7th ed. Mayfield, Mountain View, California.

Hodges, H. W. M. (ed.)
    1987   *In Situ Archaeological Conservation.* Getty Conservation Institute, Los Angeles.

Hume, I. N.
    1972   *Historical Archaeology.* Knopf, New York.
    1978   *A Guide to the Artifacts of Colonial America.* Knopf, New York.

Jones, O. R., and C. Sullivan
    1989   *The Parks Canada Glass Glossary for the Description of Containers, Tablewares, Flat Glass, and Closures.* Studies in Archaeology, Architecture and History. Canadian Park Service, Ottawa.

Joukowsky, M.
    1980   *A Complete Manual of Field Archaeology: Tools and Techniques of Field Work for Archaeologists.* Prentice Hall, Englewood Cliffs, New Jersey.

Karklins, K., and R. Sprague
    1980   *A Bibliography of Glass Trade Beads in North America.* South Fork Press, Moscow, Idaho.

Kelso, G. K., and M. C. Beaudry
    1990   Pollen Analysis and Urban Land Use: The Environs of Scottow's Dock in 17th, 18th, and Early 19th Century Boston. *Historical Archaeology* 24(1):61–81.

Kidd, K., and M. Kidd
    1970   A Classification System for Glass Beads for the Use of Field Archaeologists. *Occasional Papers in Archaeology and History* 1:45–89.

Leigh, D.
    1978   *First Aid for Finds.* Rescue 1, Hertford, England.

Longacre, J.
    1968   Some Aspects of Prehistoric Society in East-Central Arizona. In *New Perspectives in Archaeology*, S. Binford and L. Binford (eds.), pp. 89–102. Aldine, Chicago.

Lorrain, D.
    1968   An Archaeologist's Guide to 19th c. American Glass. *Historical Archaeology* 2:35–44.

Loy, T. H.
    1990   Prehistoric Organic Residues: Recent Advances in Identification, Dating and their Antiquity. In *Archaeometry '90*, W. Wagner and M. Pernicka (eds.), pp. 645–56. Birkhauser Verlag, Basel.

Lyon, E. A.
1996   *A New Deal for Southeastern Archaeology.* University of Alabama Press, Tuscaloosa.

Magoon, D. T.
1998   The Ceramics of Craftsman Robert Hay and Family: An Analysis of Middle Class Consumer-Choice in Antebellum New Bern, North Carolina. M.A. thesis, East Carolina University.

Mallowan, A. C.
1946   *Come, Tell Me How You Live.* Dodd, Mead, New York.

Miller, G. L.
1980   Classification and Economic Scaling of Nineteenth-Century Ceramics. *Historical Archaeology* 14:1–40.

Miller, G. L., and C. Sullivan
1984   Machine-Made Glass Containers and the End of Production for Mouth-Blown Bottles. *Historical Archaeology* 18(2):83–96.

Nelson, L. H.
1963   Nail Chronology as an Aid to Dating Old Buildings. *History News* 19(2).

Nesmith, R.
1955   *The Coinage of the First Mint of the Americas at Mexico City, 1536–1572.* Numismatic Notes And Monographs. American Numismatic Society, New York.

Neumann, G. C., and F. Kravic
1977   *Collector's Illustrated Encyclopedia of the American Revolution.* Castle Books, Secaucus, New Jersey.

Newman, T. S.
1970   A Dating Key for Post-18th c. Bottles. *Historical Archaeology* 4:70–75.

Oakeshott, R. E.
1960   *The Archaeology of Weapons: Arms and Armor from Prehistory to the Age of Chivalry.* Dover, New York.

Partridge, M.
1973   *Farm Tools through the Ages.* New York Graphic Society, Boston.

Quimby, G. (ed.)
1980   *Ceramics in America.* University Press of Virginia, Charlottesville.

Rice, P. M.
1987   *Pottery Analysis: A Sourcebook.* University of Chicago Press, Chicago.

Ridings, R.
    1996   Where in the World Does Obsidian Hydration Dating Work?
            American Antiquity 61(1):136–48.

Rock, J. T.
    2000   Cans in the Countryside. In *Approaches to Material Culture
            Research for Historical Archaeologists*, D. R. Brauner (ed.),
            pp. 275–89. Society for Historical Archaeology, California, Penn-
            sylvania.

Roenke, K. G.
    1978   Flat Glass: Its Use as a Dating Tool for Nineteenth Century Ar-
            chaeological Sites in the Pacific Northwest and Elsewhere.
            Northwest Anthropological Research Notes 12(2).

Rovner, I.
    1994   Floral History by the Back Door: A Test of Phytolith Analysis in
            Residential Yards at Harper's Ferry. *Historical Archaeology*
            28(4):37–48.

Sanford, E.
    1975   Conservation of Artifacts: A Question of Survival. *Historical
            Archaeology* 9:55–64.

Schiffer, Michael B. and John H. House
    1975   *The Cache River Project: An Experiment in Contract Archaeol-
            ogy*. Research Series Number 8. Arkansas Archaeological Sur-
            vey, Fayetteville, Arkansas.

Sease, C.
    1994   *A Conservation Manual for the Field Archaeologist*, 3d ed. Ar-
            chaeological Research Tools 4. Institute of Archaeology; Uni-
            versity of California, Los Angeles.

Shephard, A. O.
    1980   *Ceramics for the Archaeologist*. Publication No. 609. Carnegie
            Institute, Washington, D.C.

Shott, M. J.
    1994   Size and Form in the Analysis of Flake Debris: Review and Re-
            cent Approaches. *Journal of Archaeological Method and Theory*
            1(1):69–110.

Singley, K. R.
    1981   Caring for Artifacts after Excavation—Some Advice for Archae-
            ologists. *Historical Archaeology* 15(1):36–48.

Smith, M. T.
    1983   Chronology from Glass Beads: The Spanish Period in the South-
            east, c. A.D. 1513–1670. In *Proceedings of the 1982 Trade Bead*

Conference, Charles F. Hayes III (ed.), pp. 147–58. Research Records, vol. 16. Rochester Museum and Science Center, Rochester, New York.

Smith, M. T., and M. E. Good
1982 *Early Sixteenth-Century Beads in the Spanish Colonial Trade.* Cottonlandia Museum, Greenwood, Mississippi.

South, S.
1977 *Method and Theory in Historical Archaeology.* Academic Press, New York.

South, S., R. K. Skowronek, and R. E. Johnson
1988 *Spanish Artifacts from Santa Elena.* Occasional Papers of the South Carolina Institute of Archaeology and Anthropology, Anthropological Studies 7. University of South Carolina, Columbia.

Spaulding, A. C.
1953 Statistical Techniques for the Discovery of Artifact Types. *American Antiquity* 18:305–13.
1954 Reply (to Ford). *American Antiquity* 19(4):391–93.

Stahle, D. W., M. K. Cleaveland, D. B. Blanton, M. D. Therrell, and D. A. Gay
1998 The Lost Colony and Jamestown Droughts. *Science* 280(5363):564–67.

Sullivan, A., and K. Rozen
1985 Debitage Analysis and Archaeological Interpretation. *American Antiquity* 50(4):755–79.

Sutton, M. Q., and B. S. Arkush
1998 *Archaeological Laboratory Methods: An Introduction.* Kendall/Hunt, Dubuque, Iowa.

Switzer, R. R.
1974 *The Bertrand Bottles: A Study of Nineteenth-Century Glass and Ceramic Containers.* National Park Service, Washington, D.C.

Thomas, D. H.
1978 The Awful Truth about Statistics in Archaeology. *American Antiquity* 43(2):231–44.
1986 *Refiguring Anthropology: First Principles of Probability and Statistics.* Waveland Press, Prospect Heights, Illinois.
1998 *Archaeology,* 3d ed. Harcourt Brace, New York.

Trigger, B. G.
1989 *A History of Archaeological Thought.* Cambridge University Press, London.

Vaughn, P.
    1985   *Use-Wear Analysis of Flaked Stone Tools.* University of Arizona
            Press, Tucson.

Wells, T.
    2000   Nail Chronology: The Use of Technologically Derived Features.
            In *Approaches to Material Culture Research for Historical Ar-
            chaeologists,* D. R. Brauner (ed.), pp. 318–39. Society for Histor-
            ical Archaeology.

White, J. R.
    1978   Bottle Nomenclature: A Glossary of Landmark Terminology for
            the Archaeologist. *Historical Archaeology* 12:58–67.

Willey, G. R., and P. Phillips
    1958   *Method and Theory in American Archaeology.* University of
            Chicago Press, Chicago.

Williams, M. W.
    1986   Sub-surface Patterning at Sixteenth-Century Spanish Puerto
            Real, Haiti. *Journal of Field Archaeology* 13(3):283–96.

Winters, H. D.
    1968   Value Systems and Trade Cycles of the Late Archaic in the Mid-
            west. In *New Perspectives in Archaeology,* S. Binford and L. Bin-
            ford (eds.), pp. 175–222. Aldine, Chicago.

INDEX

ABOUT THE AUTHOR
AND SERIES EDITORS

Charles R. Ewen received his B.A. at the University of Minnesota (1978), M.A. at Florida State (1983), and Ph.D. at the University of Florida (1987). After graduation, he codirected excavations at the Governor Martin site (the site of Hernando de Soto's first winter encampment) for the Florida Bureau of Archaeological Research. The next stop was Arkansas, where he was an assistant professor and director of the Arkansas Archeological Survey's Sponsored Research Program. He joined the faculty of East Carolina University (ECU) in 1994, where he is a professor in the Anthropology Department. He also serves as director of the Phelps Archaeology Lab on the ECU campus. His research interests include archaeological method and theory, cultural resource management, and historical archaeology, specifically the Contact and Colonial periods. Like most archaeologists, however, circumstances have led him to work on nearly every kind of site, from prehistoric villages to Civil War fortifications and twentieth-century homesteads. He has established a research program in eastern North Carolina, conducting projects at Tryon Palace Historic Sites and Gardens, Hope Plantation, Historic Edenton, and the Newbold-White house.

Besides several articles and book chapters, Charlie is the author of two books about fieldwork he has conducted: *From Spaniard to Creole: The Archaeology of Cultural Formation at Puerto Real, Haiti* (University of Alabama Press, 1991) and *Hernando de Soto among the Apalachee: The Archaeology of the First Winter Encampment* (coauthor, University of Florida Press, 1998). He is currently working on a coedited volume concerning the colonies at Roanoke Island. He lives happily near the university with his wife, Gretchen, and two daughters, Kate and Madeline.

Larry J. Zimmerman is the head of the Archaeology Department of the Minnesota Historical Society. He served as an adjunct professor of anthropology and visiting professor of American Indian and Native Studies at the University of Iowa from 1996 to 2002 and as chair of the American Indian and Native Studies Program from 1998 to 2001. He earned his Ph.D. in anthropology at the University of Kansas in 1976. Teaching at the University of South Dakota for twenty-two years, he left there in 1996 as Distinguished Regents Professor of Anthropology.

While in South Dakota, he developed a major CRM program and the University of South Dakota Archaeology Laboratory, where he is still a research associate. He was named the University of South Dakota Student Association Teacher of the Year in 1980, given the Burlington Northern Foundation Faculty Achievement Award for Outstanding Teaching in 1986, and granted the Burlington Northern Faculty Achievement Award for Research in 1990. He was selected by Sigma Xi, the Scientific Research Society, as a national lecturer from 1991 to 1993, and he served as executive secretary of the World Archaeological Congress from 1990 to 1994. He has published more than three hundred articles, CRM reports, and reviews and is the author, editor, or coeditor of fifteen books, including *Native North America* (with Brian Molyneaux, University of Oklahoma Press, 2000) and *Indians and Anthropologists: Vine Deloria, Jr., and the Critique of Anthropology* (with Tom Biolsi, University of Arizona Press, 1997). He has served as the editor of *Plains Anthropologist* and the *World Archaeological Bulletin* and as the associate editor of *American Antiquity*. He has done archaeology in the Great Plains of the United States and in Mexico, England, Venezuela, and Australia. He has also worked closely with a wide range of American Indian nations and groups.

William Green is Director of the Logan Museum of Anthropology and Adjunct Professor of Anthropology at Beloit College, Beloit, Wisconsin. He has been active in archaeology since 1970. Having grown up on the south side of Chicago, he attributes his interest in archaeology and anthropology to the allure of the exotic (i.e., rural) and a driving urge to learn the unwritten past, abetted by the opportunities available at the city's museums and universities. His first field work was on the Mississippi River bluffs in western Illinois. Although he also worked in Israel and England, he returned to Illinois for several years of survey and excavation. His interests in settlement patterns, ceramics, and archaeobotany developed there. He received his Master's degree from the University of Wisconsin–Madison and then served as Wisconsin SHPO staff archaeologist for eight years. After obtaining his Ph.D. from UW–Madison in 1987, he served as State Archaeologist of Iowa from 1988 to 2001, directing statewide research and service programs including burial site protection, geographic information, publications, contract services, public outreach, and curation. His main research interests focus on the development and spread of native agriculture. He has served as editor of the *Midcontinental Journal of Archaeology* and *The Wisconsin Archeologist*, has published articles in *American Antiquity*, *Journal of Archaeological Research*, and other journals, and has received grants and contracts from the National Science Foundation, National Park Service, Iowa Humanities Board, and many other agencies and organizations.

CPSIA information can be obtained
at www.ICGtesting.com
Printed in the USA
LVHW031728101219
640063LV00014B/1069/P

9 780759 100220